AF605945

THE CATHOLIC UNIVERSITY OF AMERICA
CANON LAW STUDIES
Number 70

CHURCH LAW ON SACRED RELICS

A DISSERTATION

Submitted to the Faculty of Canon Law of the Catholic University of America in Partial Fulfillment of the Requirements for the Degree of

DOCTOR OF CANON LAW

BY

EUGENE A. DOOLEY, J. C. L.
Oblate of Mary Immaculate

THE CATHOLIC UNIVERSITY OF AMERICA
WASHINGTON, D. C.
1931

Nihil Obstat:

GULIELMUS W. NOONAN, O.M.I., J.C.D.

Imprimi Potest:

TERENTIUS W. SMITH, O.M.I., D.D.

Nihil Obstat:

VALENTINUS SCHAAF, O.F.M., J.C.D.,
Censor Deputatus.

Washingtonii, D. C., die XXI Maii, 1931.

Imprimatur:

✠ MICHAELIS J. CURLEY, D.D.,
Archiepiscopus Baltimorensis.

Baltimoriac, die XIII Maii, 1931.

WASHINGTON TYPOGRAPHERS, INC.
WASHINGTON, D. C.

TABLE OF CONTENTS

FOREWORD

The standard English work on the cult of Relics in the Catholic Church has not yet been written. This monograph is a canonical study of the cult, not intended as the complete story but merely as a canonical guide to the right observance today. It seemed to the writer that a complete story of the devotion could not be written in America, because many important documents and catalogues repose in European libraries.

Few books have been written explicitly on the cult of Relics, but nevertheless there is plenty of material extant. The best practical story of the devotion is in the Italian language, *Il Culto delle Reliquie,* by Mioni. The *Tractatus Orthodoxus de Sanctorum Ss. Reliquiis* by Agricola is a good treatise in Latin, but it is antiquated. The older theologians, both in Moral and Dogmatic Theology, discussed Relics also. Lugo has the best treatment of the veneration from the viewpoint of Moral Theology; Reiffenstuel excels from the viewpoint of Canon Law; and Bellarmine excels from the aspect of dogmatic and apologetic controversy. Mabillon has given many sound rules for the authentication of Relics, but Honoratus a Sancta Maria has gone much farther in this precise matter, and has drawn up principles which are as perfect in this study as can ever be desired. Zallwein in his *Principia Juris Ecclesiastici* of the eighteenth century is thorough and exact. Of the more recent authors, Perrone is the most original and thorough, while Craisson also has excellent matter. Barbier de Montault has likewise written many excellent treatises on Relics.

All books on Liturgy have rules for the right care and exposition of Relics of the Saints. Most of these regulations have been culled from the numerous decrees issued by the Congregation of Rites and the Congregation of Indulgences and Relics.

In the English language, the only explicit treatment of Relics, apart from occasional articles in periodicals or pamphlets, is in the articles of encyclopedias. Of all these, Hastings *Encyclopedia of Religion and Ethics* gives the best historical outline, but it lacks the Catholic attitude for the cult, and hence, is unsatisfactory. In French, the *Dictionnaire Apologétique de la Foi Catholique* has the best summary sketch of the devotion, but the *Analecta Bollandiana* has numerous articles on individual relics which are well presented. Sources in the German language add nothing to those in the French. Beissel in his *Verehrung der Heiligen und ihrer Reliquien in Deutschland* and Pfister in his *Der Reliquienkult im Altertum* are rather historical than canonical.

The new Code of Canon Law has taken from the multicplicity of laws in the past less than a dozen canons, but these are so well worded and so comprehensive in their extent that they leave little to be desired. In these days there has been a rekindling of devotion to Saints and their relics, and there has been the consequent desire to know what the laws of the Church prescribe in this matter. The intention of satisfying that desire in some small way has motivated this writing. The point of view has been mainly canonical. Dogmatic and moral truths that underlie the cult have not been treated at any length; rather have the canonical rules for the observance of the discipline and the cult been considered and stressed, always with the view of presenting something positive and practical rather than truths merely speculative and theories mainly intellectual. The task has not been easy, because of the necessity of combining caution, circumspection and prudence with the principles of sound criticism. The study of the cult of Sacred Relics has so many intricacies" ". . . that even learned and excellent authors who wrote explicitly on the subject have sometimes *increased, created and multiplied* the difficulties."[1]

The first part of this work is a historical sketch of the growth of laws concerning sacred Relics; the second part is a commentary on the laws in the Code which concern these sacred objects.

In quotations from the Fathers, the Migne edition has been used; the English translations have been made by the present author, except where the contrary is expressly stated.

---

[1] Zallwein, *Principia Juris Ecclesiastici,* II, 139.

The author expresses sincere thanks to his religious superiors because of their constant encouragement and assistance. To the professors in the Canon Law faculty at the University he is exceedingly grateful. Without their cooperation, this monograph could not have appeared, and consequently it stands as a tribute to their unfailing kindness.

PART I

THE CULT OF RELICS BEFORE THE CODE OF CANON LAW

CHAPTER I

THE NATURE OF RELICS

ART. 1. DEFINITIONS OF THE WORD

The English word *relic* corresponds to the Latin word *reliquiae*, and to the Greek word *λείψανα*. All of them bear the same meaning—some fragment of a thing lost or destroyed.

In the ecclesiastical usage of the word, the first meaning of *relic* signifies the actual remains of the bodies of the saints. This includes the whole body or parts of it, or the remains of the body after death. The second meaning of the word embraces all those things which the saint used while alive, or things which were sanctified by their contact with him. Included in this are the clothes or the garments of the saint, or the cloths in which the body was wrapped after death. The third and final signification of the word *relic* includes all other physical objects which have been applied to, or closely associated with, all the relics in the other two classes.[1]

---

[1] De Lugo, *Disputationes Scholasticae, De Incarnatione,* disp. XXXVII, sect. 1—". . . Honor enim et cultus qui reliquiis exhibetur, non est cultus vulgaris, sed peculiaris quidam honor, qui tribuitur aliquibus rebus propter peculiarem connexionem quam habent cum Deo vel Sanctis, quales sunt vestes, instrumenta passionis, loca in quibus aliquid peculiare operati sunt, ex quo fit ut non possit haberi prudenter pro reliquia alicuius Sancti, pars terrae illius civitatis, in qua habitavit, quia licet tota illa civitas habeat aliquam connexionem cum illo Sancto, non tamen tam peculiarem, qualis requiritur ad hoc, ut habeatur et adoretur ut reliquia: posset tamen assumi ut reliquia, aliqua pars cubiculi in quo diu habitavit. Quod si Sanctus ille habitasset in pluribus civitatibus, et in singulis cubiculis cuiusque civitatis, non haberetur pro reliquia pars cuiusque civitatis, quia ad cultum reliquiae exigunt homines aliquam peculiarem connexionem cum Sancto, cum autem tunc connexio illa non esset peculiaris cuivis cubiculo, sed communis cum aliis innumeris, hinc est, in communi prudentum aestimatione, non debere illam haberi, nec coli cultu peculiari, qui reliquiis exhibetur, qui sine dubio maior est quam cultus exhibitus cuilibet alteri rei. . . ."

Cf. also, Suarez, *Disputationes,* LV sect. 1; Vasquez, *Disp.* CXII, cap. LV—maintaining that only objects closely related to the Saints are true relics.

This natural division of all relics into three classes corresponds to the relations of nearness or proximity to the person of the saint. The closer the relationship, the more noteworthy is the relic. In the Migne *Encyclopedie Théologique,*[2] these divisions have been called by the clumsy terms: relics *properly so-called,* relics *less properly so-called,* and relics *improperly so-called. . .* A better terminology calls these relics *primary, secondary* and *tertiary.*[3]

Perhaps the best of all terms, however, are those in the common usage today, which, though mentioned by hardly one author, came into existence because of their conciseness and precision. According to this terminology, relics are either *first-class, second-class* or *third-class,* depending on whether they are actual parts of a body, parts of the garments actually worn by the saints, or articles which have come into contact with any in the former classes. All the bone-particles of the body are first-class relics; the garments, clothes, books of the saint, and the instruments used in inflicting death on a martyr are second-class; all other things which have come into direct contact with the above are third-class. These last have been properly called relics of contact, and they are the last and lowest class of relics. No further extension is allowed.[4]

These divisions are based on natural physical partitions or association. Legally, however, the Church does not recognize any but two classes. According to the Code of Canon Law, there are only two kinds of relics: *insignes* and *non-insignes,* or, in English, *notable* and *non-notable.* The Code does not mention the fact that relics of the True Cross or of the Passion are notable, but this is certain from decrees of the Congregation of Rites and the Congregation of Relics where special and distinctive honors were attributed to them.[5]

---

[2] Volume 26, col. 1073 seq.

[3] Augustine, *A Commentary,* VI, 91; Woywod, "The Law of the Code on Altars," *The Homiletic and Pastoral Review, XXVI* (1925), 265; Many, *Praelectiones de Locis Sacris,* p. 208.

[4] De Lugo, *loc cit.,* maintaining that association or propinquity is the basis for the natural classifications of relics. Any relic farther removed from the saint than a third-class relic is not a relic at all.

[5] S. R. C., Decretum Generale, May 27, 1826—*Decr. Auth.,* n. 2647 and S. C. Indulg, et Reliq., *Coenomanen,* Feb. 22, 1847—*Decr. Auth.,* n. 342,

Canon 1281 reads thus:

> Notable relics of the Saints and Blessed are the entire body, or the head, arm, forearm, heart, tongue, hand, leg, or that part of the body in which the martyr suffered, provided that it be entire and not small.

Augustine in his Commentary[6] translates *"insignis"* as *important.* Woywod prefers the word *prominent.*[7] Both words are correct to a certain extent, but neither corresponds precisely to the strict meaning of *"insignis."* The best English word would be *remarkable,* but that would denote an idea of extraordinary or strange character in a relic, and such is not the intent of the Code. In the absence of a better word, *"notable"* seems to be the most appropriate. It is better than the others because it implies *prominence* and *importance,* as well as a further idea that the relic is possessed of an additional characteristic that marks it out as distinct and separate from the ordinary smaller relics. Notable relics are complete members of a body, and hence are more noteworthy than mere parts of it.

All notable relics are *first-class,* since all of them are actual parts of a saint's body. Not all *first-class* relics, however, are notable, since many of them are small in size and dimension. It is safe to say that very few churches in America at present possess a notable relic. In the great majority of cases, the most they possess is a *first-class* relic.

De Lugo demands another element in a thing besides association with a saint before it can be a relic in public devotions. This element he terms *decency.*

---

ruling that relics of the True Cross are to be kept separate from other relics of the Saints. Cf. S. R. C., *Ordinis Minorum,* Sept. 17, 1897—*Decr. Auth.,* n. 3966, demanding the same honors for the Crown of Thorns. De Herdt, *Sacrae Liturgiae Praxis,* II, n. 197, expressly states that there are two classes of *"reliquiae insignes."* In the first class are notable relics of the Saints; in the second are the wood of the Cross, the Crown of Thorns, and the other instruments of the Passion. Honors paid to relics in either class are not communicable to the other, De Herdt says. Cavalieri, *Opera Omnia Liturgica,* I, decr. 51, denies this latter, and maintains that all honors paid to relics of the Saints may be paid to those of the Passion, but not vice-versa.

[6] *A Commentary,* VI, 244.

[7] *The New Canon Law,* p. 263. Wuest, *Matters Liturgical,* n. 802, also chooses this term.

> That thing which is held and cherished as a relic not only ought to be a thing pertaining to the saint, but also ought to be of such a nature that it contain nothing of turpitude, by which the cult would be rendered indecent here and now. Wherefore all theologians teach that the ass which Christ used to enter Jerusalem could not be honored as a relic because that cult, by reason of the subject, would be indecent. The same is to be said about other things also. . . . Who would venerate as relics the heretical books that Augustine wrote before his conversion? . . . Some things which had peculiar relationship and contact with Christ cannot decently be honored on account of their indignity and indecency, . . . such as the hand of the person who struck Him (during the Passion) . . . Thus on account of similar indecency, the lips of Judas, if they should still exist, could not be honored.[8]

This requirement of a certain fitness in the relic purifies the devotion and raises a legal bar against those relics surely associated with a saint but associated in such a way that they do not serve to arouse religious sentiments concerning him. Pius X enunciated the same view in the encyclical letter *"Pascendi,"* telling Bishops that in the cult of relics a Christian moderation is to be used, as well as respect and decorum. Tact and foresight were encouraged by the Pope, so that no relic would be approved which would make the cult ridiculous or despicable.[9]

ART. 2. RELIC CULT IN RELATION TO PAGANISM

There is a sharp and clear-cut distinction between the savage-magic of the pagan fetishes and the veneration of relics in the Catholic faith.[10] This point is important, though many writers not friendly to the Church are inclined to overlook it, or to minimize it, by dogmatically attributing to the Church vague beliefs and assumed theories which are far from true and right.[11]

---

[8] *Disputationes Scholasticae, De Incarnatione,* XXXVII, sect. III.

[9] *Acta Pontificia,* V, 373; *Acta Sanctae Sedis,* XL, 593; Sporer-Bierbaum, *Theologia Moralis,* I, n. 293.

[10] *Dict. Apolog. de la Foi Cath.,* art. *Magie,* III, 66; Mioni, *Il Culto delle Reliquie,* chapters I and XII; many of the Fathers wrote on this point, and their testimony will be brought in later, on page 14 ss. St. Jerome, especially, gave express consideration to this matter.

[11] There is a school in the field of Comparative Theology which sees in relic cult only another manifestation of surviving (pagan) ideas. Dele-

The instinct of the human heart is to hold in veneration and respect the memory of a dead friend, or some great character. That is a natural tendency, common to all men and all peoples. The manner and the mode in which this veneration is manifested will vary with changed conditions, and there can be tremendous differences between one cult and another. On the one hand, any rank superstition which puts into the bones or the vesture of a dead person the self-same mystic current of strength and virtue which the person possessed during life may be discarded at once, as unworthy of credence by any true thinker. Such beliefs are at the bottom of all magic and superstition and fetishisms, in attributing to a merely material thing some power and action surpassing its physical nature.

Then, on the other hand, there is nothing unnatural or reprehensible in that mere human veneration for the dead person, strengthened by the consideration of what that person did during life. It is quite natural to remember, and to admire the deeds of friends of the past.

In our Faith, the veneration of relics falls into neither of these classes completely. It is unique. It avoids the degenerate excess of savage magic or pagan fetishism, and it supplies the timid deficiencies of mere spiritual symbolism. Relics are extraordinary things, but of themselves, they have no mystic causal forces. They are symbols also, but they are not mere symbols. They are material particles, souvenirs, or tokens, representing the personality of some hero of the Faith who proved himself so worthy a follower of Christ that it is fit and right to honor his memory before the material vestige of his relic. The terminus of the cult is not the physical object, but the person to whom that object originally belonged; and even then, the object of the cult is not the human being, but rather God, who is honored

---

haye, in *Legends of the Saints*, p. 160-168, treats this question well. The prevailing hostility toward the value of the cult, as found expressed in the popular editions of the *Encyclopedia Britannica*, XX, 355, the *Jewish Encyclopedia*, XXIII, 59, and *La Grande Encyclopedie*, XXVIII, 367, may all be traced back to the writings of the Madgeburg Centuriators, after the Protestant Reformation in the sixteenth century. Bellarmine, *De Controversiis Christianae Fidei*, II, 463-473, analyzes and evaluates their assertions.

through the medium of the person faithful to Him. The cult of relics finds its absolute terminus in God; it uses the relative agency of a material thing to show forth its reverence.

Religious instincts are common to all men, and it is to be expected that there will be found resemblances and similarities in the religions of all peoples, though they be miles apart in their beliefs. Plutarch told with great gusto about the honors that were paid to the relics of Theseus. Translations of heroes in the pagan past were carried out with ceremonies very similar to those used in the Christian translations of relics in the early days of the Church. The honors paid to the relics of Orestes, Oedipus, Phocion and Demetrius are very much like those paid to the relics of Christian saints,—so much alike, that some writers have called the Christian cult a mere pagan survival. The theory is specious, but the only things proved by it are facts that everyone admits: namely, that all men at all times have had religious instincts and reverence for the great ones of the past. Delehaye has dwelt upon this question, and he has summarized the truth of the matter in these justly famous words:

> The history of the two cults [. . . that is, of the pagan and Christian relics] represents a logical and parallel development, without, however, any mutual interdependence. . . . They are the natural outcome of an identical state of the mind under similar circumstances.[12]

Perrone adds another note to the ideas of Delehaye, by stating that ceremonies and rites are materially indifferent in themselves, taking their main morality from the object, the circumstances and the motive. In the Christian cult, he says,[13] the object and the motive differ. Nor does the similarity or even the material identity of rites argue any necessity that the Christian cult be accused of superstition or idolatry. Even in the supposition that the Catholic cult were borrowed from the pagan rites, (which is not true) there are still enough of intrinsic differences in it to change its whole nature. Because one cult followed the other is no reason to say that the first caused the

[12] Delehaye, *Legends of the Saints*, p. 166. Cf. *Dict. Théol. Cath.*, art. *Magie*, IX, 1534, for another excellent treatment of the same point,—i.e., similarity being no argument for identity.

[13] Perrone, *Praelectiones Theologicae*, II, 433, n. 102.

second. *Post hoc, ergo propter hoc* is neither good logic, nor good theology. Similarity does not argue for descendancy.

ART. 3. CAUSAL FORCES IN A RELIC

The element of miracle-causality has never been defined or explained by explicit statements of the Church. St. Thomas Aquinas said that God worked miracles ". . . *in their presence*," and this apparently supposes that the relic is not the cause of the miracle, but rather the occasion or the condition for it.[14] The Council of Trent stated that relics were agencies ". . . *through which* . . . " God worked prodigies.[15] Any attempts to read into these expressions the notion of physical or intrinsic causality can be nothing more than guesses or assumptions.

Some of the Fathers, especially Saint Cyril of Jerusalem, are quoted as if they held for a physical causative force inherent in the relics, but the passages cited are rather oratorical imagery or rhetorical endeavors to honor the Saints, than cool and systematic treatises on the nature of the causality.[16] In other passages, Saint Cyril makes it clear that he was not a fanatical preacher of a magic power coursing through the relics, after the supposed fashion of a pagan charm or talisman.

---

[14] *Summa Theologica,* III, q. 25, art. 6, *Utrum reliquiae sanctorum sint adorandae.* St. Thomas deals with the question of superstition in the wearing of relics on one's person, in the *Summa,* II, IIae, q. 96, art. 4, ad 3um, and says that ". . . if they be worn out of confidence in God and in the Saints whose relics they are, it will not be unlawful. But if account were taken of some vain circumstance (for instance, that the casket be three-cornered, or the like, having no bearing on the reverence due to God and the Saints), it would be superstitious and unlawful."

[15] Sess. XXV, *De invocatione, veneratione, et reliquiis sanctorum, et sacris imaginibus.*

[16] Many authors treat this point, but the best is Thurston, "Relics," *Cath. Encycl.,* XII, 735. The words of St. Cyril are as follows: ". . . Non solum anima sanctorum honoretur credaturque; in corporibus mortuorum inest virtus, seu potentia jacens . . ."—*Catech.,* 18:16—*MPG,* XXXIII, 1070 ss. Lucius, a Protestant theologian, in *Le Culte des Saints,* pp. 167-180, has compiled an imposing list of phrases used by the Fathers, all of which seem to indicate that they were believers in a mystic current of causal power, residing in the relics of Saints. The *Encyclopedia of Religion and Ethics,* X, 654, trembles for the orthodoxy of the same Fathers.

CHAPTER II

HISTORY OF LEGISLATION ON THE CULT

ART. 1. THE START OF THE VENERATION

No one knows who was the first person to venerate relics. It is so natural a thing, that it is extremely doubtful whether anyone will ever be able to trace and find out the first devotee.[1] There was no positive law which mentioned relics until the year 401, and there was no explicit law which advocated their cult until the year 787, in the second Council of Nicea. There were general customs and practises by the people, and preaching by the bishops, but no express and explicit law. It was a natural devotion, arising out of some yearning or craving in our personality to cherish memories and friendship. Bellarmine says[2] in answer to some objections of the Calvinists on this score that it was not a purely human devotion, established and perfected by men alone, but was inspired by God.

Christ healed the woman who touched "only the hem of His garment." This was in accord with the Catholic idea that physical and material things are the channels and the agencies for God's works towards mankind.[3] The Apostle Paul was the medium that God used later on, to perform similar prodigies. Handkerchiefs and aprons that had touched his person were

---

[1] Perrone, *Praelectiones Theologicae,* II, 428 and 432, states that the cult of relics, in practice, is inseparable from the cult of the martyrs themselves. He proves the existence of devotion to relics in the first three centuries by the solicitude in collecting relics even at the risk of life, by the monuments and memorials erected over the graves, by the zeal in separating martyrs' graves from others, and finally by the honors paid at their tombs (Mass, Eucharist, prayers, kissing of relics). Cf. also Mioni, *Il Culto Delle Reliquie,* cap. 1; Bouvier, *Institutiones Theologicae,* II, 242; Bellarmine, *De Controversiis Christianae Fidei,* II, 470; *Dict. Apolog. de la Foi Cath.,* IV, 909.

[2] Bellarmine, *De Controversiis,* II, 471, *ad 3um;* Sporer-Bierbaum, *Theol. Moralis,* I, 465, n. 298.

[3] Newman, *Essay on Development of Christian Doctrine,* p. 370.

brought to the diseased, and their sicknesses were healed. Even the shadow of St. Peter had the force of an intermediary agency in the cure of the sick,—and surely there are few things less real than a shadow.[4] But all this did not begin at the time of Christ. There is continuity in this matter between the Old Law and the New Law, because there are other places in the sacred writings which show that in times past, God has worked miracles through the agency of inanimate objects which were honored as relics.[5] Faith in the power of God and the ready willingness to believe that He will exert His Providence through His creatures both combine with the natural instincts of cherishing remembrance, and all these tend to show how the cult arose.

There was a strong tendency from the earliest days of the Church to have Mass celebrated only at places where there were relics of martyrs, and it is quite certainly established that the first altars used for the celebration of the Eucharist were these tombs of martyrs.[6] Very often, the bodies of martyrs were buried in niches that had been cut out of the passage-way in the Catacombs. The bodies in these niches were covered with a

---

[4] *Matthew* 9:21; *Acts* 19:12 and 5:15.

[5] *IV Kings*, 2:14 and 13:21. Apart from these two places, there are many other places telling of the cult of relics in the Old Law, where God did not work miracles, but where the people venerated relics of their patriarchs and prophets. Murray, *De Veneratione Sanctorum*, p. 53, n. 117 seq., recalls the purpose of relic veneration. They are honored, not because miracles are done through them, or have been done through them in the past—though in such cases the veneration is more intense and fervent—but rather because *they are* the relics of saints. Their honor is the primary object, not personal utility or profit.

[6] Duchesne, *Liber Pontificalis*, I, 185, attributes to Pope Felix I [269-274] a decree that Mass was to be said on tombs of martyrs. Baronius, *ad annum 275*, n. 2, tom. 3, p. 195, says that this was a law, even before Felix I. So also say the Bollandists, *Acta Ss. Aprilis*, I, 23, and Tillemont, *Historia Ecclesiastica*, IV, 364. That there were altars over the relics of saints is certain. Cf. De Rossi, *Roma Sotterranea*, III, 489; Marucchi, *Evidences for the Catacombs*, p. 29; Northcote, *Roman Catacombs*, p. 58; Gihr, *The Mass*, p. 328; Bliley, *Altars*, p. 36. The Fathers give explicit testimony on this. Cf. St. Ambrose, Epist. XXII, *Ad Marcellinum*, *MPL*, 16:1019—". . . no consecration of church or altar without relics present. . . ." Also St. Ambrose, *Exhortatio Virginum*, II, 10, *MPL*, XVI, 1600; St. Augustine, *Sermo 336 de Sanctis*, *MPL*, XXXVIII, 1471; Paulinus, *Poem.* 19 and 26, *MPL*, LXI, 511 and 640. Bliley, *loc. cit.*, does not admit any certain proving value in the purported decree of Felix I as above, asserting that it told of a practice, not a law.

stone slab, and it was this stone which served as a table for the Sacrifice of the Mass. When the martyr was notable, more of the passage-way would be excavated, and often a chapel would be carved out in front of the grave, so that many people could hear Mass at the place of the martyr's relics.[7]

St. John in the Apocalypse (6:19) said that he saw under the altars the souls of them that were slain for the Word of God. Some deny that this refers to the practise of putting relics under the altars;[8] other Catholic writers, however, maintain that it is the narration of a fact, open and evident, even in the days of Saint John.[9]

But even apart from all this, there is clear testimony of honor being paid to relics, as early as the year 107 A. D. In that year, St. Ignatius was thrown to the wild beasts in the Roman amphitheatre, and in the Acts of that Saint there is told the story of the recovery and the veneration of the remains. There is narrated, also, the time and circumstances of meeting at the tomb ". . . to honor the champion and the noble martyr of Christ."[10]

Sometime about the year 169 (the exact date is uncertain), St. Polycarp was martyred. An enemy, Nicetas by name, knew of the avidity with which the Christians always collected the relics, and so he asked the Roman governor not to allow the Christians to have the dead body of the Saint, " . . . lest they forsake him that was crucified, and worship this one."[11] Nicetas

---

[7] Prudentius, in his famous verses on the passion of St. Hippolytus, said that the tomb of this martyr was an altar where the Bread of Life was distributed to the faithful who dwelt along the banks of the Tiber. *Peristephanon,* Hymn. XI—*MPL,* LX, 548-549.

[8] Beausobre, *Histoire Critique des Manichées* (2 vols., Amsterdam, 1734-1739), lib. 9, cap. 4.

[9] Bergier, *Dict. de Théologie,* VII, 152.

[10] *Martyrium Sancti et Sacri Martyris Ignatii Theophori,* in *Sanctorum Patrum Opuscula Selecta* (Oenipotenti, 1870), XIII, 67. In that place his relics were called ". . . thesaurus inaestimabilis ob martyris gratiam sanctae Ecclesiae relictam. . . ."

[11] *Acta S. Polycarpi,* cap. 16 and 18—*MPG,* V, 1043. Benedict XIV, *De Servorum Dei Beatificatione et (Beatorum) Canonizatione,* lib. I, cap. 2. Bellarmine, *De Controversiis,* II, 464, shows how the Madgeburg Centuriators contradicted themselves in assigning the origin of the cult of relics to the fifth century, when their story of the second century told of the Christians gathering the relics of St. Polycarp . . . *incredibili aviditate,* ". . . as if they were more precious than the rarest gems, and more

won his point and Roman soldiers were commanded to burn the body, but even so, the Christians salvaged the relics from the fire. They took up the bones of the saint, " . . . more precious than the most exquisite jewels," and deposited them in a fit place, where the faithful used to gather on the anniversary of his martyrdom, " . . . in memory of all the martyrs, and for the exercising of those yet to walk in his steps."[12]

The *Acta Sancti Cypriani,* written by Pontianus, a deacon, tells of the faithful spreading towels and cloths about the body of St. Cyprian after his martyrdom, so as to retrieve his blood which had been shed for Christ.[13]

Julian the Apostate, in his book against the Christians, reproached the Christians of the first century for honoring the tombs of St. Peter and St. Paul, and for praying to God at their tombs.[14] All these testify to the existence of a cult in the first centuries, and during the first days of persecution.

When the Church became free in the fourth century, there came a great change in all the ecclesiastical ceremonies. Heretofore, the Church had been a secret and hidden society; but after the Edict of Milan, it was a public and spiritual organization with a social and a sacred mission. In all the dark days of persecution, the Church had kept the precious lists of the martyrs, waiting for the glad day of freedom to honor in public the heroes of the Cross.[15] With the liberation of the Church,

---

desirable than the purest gold." The Jews and the pagans thought that the Christians adored the relics, and the *Acta S. Polycarpi* quoted here mention and refute this very explicitly.

[12] *Acta S. Polycarpi, loc. cit.* Cf. also Devoti, *Institutiones Canonicae,* I, 494, n. 3, noting that this is the constant attitude of the Church toward relics. "Eadem nunc est, quae semper fuit, Ecclesiae mens, cum Sanctorum cultum venerationemque proponit." Eusebius, *Hist. Eccles.,* V, cap. 3, tells of other incidents where pagans burned the relics of martyrs, and cast away their ashes. Bellarmine, *op. cit.,* II, 464a, rebukes the Calvinists for doing the same in the year 1562, when the relics of St. Irenaus, St. Hilary and St. Martin were destroyed.

[13] *Acta S. Cypriani,* cap. 16—*MPL,* III, 1496, shows the intensity of the desires to have some relic of that saint. "Nihil aliud ambiebat . . . quam ut proficiscentis ad Deum martyris sudores jam sanguineos possideret."

[14] St. Cyril, *Adversus Julianum,* vi—*MPG,* LXXVI, 812; Bergier, *op. cit.,* VII, 154.

[15] *Dict. Apolog. de la Foi Cath.,* IV, 911.

the cult of relics began in real earnest. Local lists of martyrs were combined and fused into one large martyrology; the secret meetings of the Christians ended, and great pilgrimages came to the tombs on the anniversary days of the martyrs. There are extant many sermons preached by the bishops on occasions such as these, and from these orations may be drawn a schematic summary of dogmatic and canonical rules on the true nature and extent of the cult.[16]

Often the bodies of the martyrs were translated from their place of burial to their former homes. This gave rise to those splendid processions of honor, known as the translations of relics.[17] As early as the fourth century, relics of the True Cross were spread throughout the world.[18]

When it is remembered that in the Jewish law it was con-

---

[16] "Honoro in cineribus semina aeternitatis; honoro corpus, quod mihi Dominum ostendit diligere,—quod me, propter Dominum, mortem docuit non timere. Cur autem non honorent corpus illud fideles, quod reverentur et daemones? . . . Honoro itaque corpus quod Christum honoravit in gladio, quod cum Christo regnabit in caelo."—St. Ambrose, sermo 93, *de Sanctis Nazario et Celso,—MPL,* XVII, 719. Cf. also St. John Chrysostom, *sermo de Sanctis Juventio et Maximo, MPG,* L, 571; St. Ambrose, Epistle XXII,—*MPL,* XVI, 1019; St. Augustine, *de martyre S. Cypriano, De Diversis,* CCCXIII, 5—*MPL,* XXXVIII, 1424.

[17] St. Jerome, *Contra Vigilantium,* V—*MPL,* XXIII, 345, tells of translation in the time of Constantine, when the relics of Saints Andrew, Luke and Timothy were brought to Constantinople. The relics were carried in vessels of gold by bishops. Magnificent processions accompanied the transfer of relics, with the people of each town forming an escort to the borders of the next town. This was done all the way from Palestine to Chalcedon. Cf. also Bellarmine, *De Controversiis,* II, 469b. Other translations of glory and splendor are mentioned by St. John Chrysostom, *Liber de S. Babyla, MPG,* XLI, 527. Cf. Theodoret, *Hist. Eccl.,* V, 36—*MPG,* LXXXII, 1206, on the translation of relics of St. Chrysostom.

[18] St. Cyril, *Catech.* X, 19—*MPG,* XXXIII, 685b: "There are many true testimonies of Christ. . . . Such is the Holy Wood of the Cross, which is seen among us even to the present day." The Migne edition has a note with many corroboratory evidences of this fact. Cf. also St. John Chrysostom, Homilia, *Quod Christus sit Deus,* 10—*MPG,* XLVIII, 826: "Why do all seek that wood on which the Sacred Body suffered and was crucified? Why do many men and women enclose its particles in gold, and wear it around their necks for ornament? . . . Because the Cross, a horrible symbol of malediction to all, can do all things after the death of the Crucified upon it. . . ." Cf. St. Gregory of Tours, *De Gloria Martyrum,* I, 5—*MPL,* LXXI, 709, telling the story of St. Helena finding the Cross in 326, and distributing relics of it which caused many marvels.

sidered as an unclean act to touch the bodies of the dead, the honor paid to the relics of the martyrs and saints takes on an added significance and a newer aspect. St. Basil spoke about this precise point, and he showed that in the Old Law the person who touched a relic of the dead was unclean, while in the New Law the person who touches a relic of the saints is blessed.[19] St. Gregory Nazianzen thundered against Julian the Apostate, and said that the blood of the martyrs could do all that the martyrs themselves could do while on earth.[20]

The veneration paid to relics of Saints by the early Christians had caused an opinion to grow among pagans that the martyrs were new gods. St. Jerome shattered this error, and set forth not merely a dogmatic response but a canonical discipline as well. "We do not worship, we do not adore . . . the relics of martyrs, but we honor them, that we may the better honor Him whose martyrs they are." [21] This was written in answer to Vigilantius, an apostate priest from Barcelona in the fourth century, who spoke and wrote vehemently against many Catholic practises, and in a particular way, the cult of martyrs and their relics.[22]

---

[19] St. Basil, *Homily on Psalm 115—MPG,* XXX, 111: ". . . When anyone died as a Jew, all his remains were deathly. When death comes for Christ, precious are the remains of His saints. Formerly, it was said to the priests and those dedicated to God: One will not (i.e., must not) be contaminated by any dead thing. Now, whoever touches a relic of a martyr receives some blessing from the grace residing in the body." Cf. also Bellarmine, *De Controversiis,* II, 465.

[20] *Contra Julianum—MPG,* XXXV, 589.

[21] St. Jerome, *Ad Riparium—MPL,* XXII, 907; *Contra Vigilantium,* IV—*MPL,* XXIII, 339-352. ". . . Vigilantius weeps and laments that relics are covered with rare cloths, and not preserved in rags or coarse cloths or thrown into the dunghill. . . . Are we sacrilegious when we enter the basilicas of the Apostles? Was Emperor Constantine sacrilegious when carrying to Constantinople the relics of Andrew, Luke and Timothy?" Bellarmine, *op. cit.,* II, 465, had the same error in mind when he wrote, "At quis unquam Catholicorum reliquias invocant? Quis unquam auditus est in precibus aut litaniis dixisse: *Sancte Reliquiae, orate pro me?* Et quis easdem unquam divino honore affecit, vel Christi loco adoravit? Nos enim reliquias quidem honoramus, et osculamur ut sacra pignora patronorum nostrorum: sed nec honoramus ut Deum, nec invocamus ut sanctos, sed minore cultu veneramur quam sanctorum spiritus, nedum quam Deum ipsum."

[22] The writings of Vigilantius have not survived the passing of the

In our days, Harnack has written in the same vein as Vigilantius, lamenting the fact that no Father of the Church condemned the "offensive worship of relics," even though the Manicheans and other cultured heathens made violent attacks upon the veneration. He ridiculed the Church for obstinacy in holding to the cult, and he charges all the Fathers, "even the Cappadocians," for allowing it to continue.[23]

On the other hand, there is Leibnitz who defends the theory and the practise of the cult. His testimony is worth presenting in full, because of his ideas on false relics.

> . . . It is not necessary to add much on the subject of relics. From the example of the bones of Eliseus, it is certain that God has worked miracles through their instrumentality. As we have proved, therefore, that provided certain limits be observed, the Saints may lawfully be venerated, it follows that it must be lawful to esteem relics also, and to take occasion from their presence, no less than from that of images, to venerate the person to whom they belong. And as it is an affair which alone depends on private affection, it does not matter although the relics which are believed to be real should happen, in point of fact, to be supposititious. We must be cautious, however, lest, by imprudent devotion, we expose ourselves to ridicule and the Church to contempt, with "them that are without"; and we should always remember, that it is our duty to act in such a way as to show that these accessories of piety do not unduly occupy our mind, nor divert it from the worship of the one Omnipotent God, which alone is of primary and supreme importance, and in comparison of which it is better to neglect all the rest than to depart from it in any particular whatsoever.[24]

St. Augustine preached the true theory of veneration, giving a beautiful exposition of the right worship.[25]

---

centuries, but his arguments can be learned from the work of St. Jerome. Another enemy of the cult, Eunomius by name, is mentioned by St. Jerome in the same book against Vigilantius, but nothing more is known about him. Cf. *Contra Vigilantium,* II—*MPL,* XXIII, 330; Bellarmine, *De Controversiis,* II, 465.

[23] Harnack, *History of Dogmas,* IV, 313.

[24] Leibnitz, *System of Theology,* p. 88; Perrone, *Praelect.,* II, 435, n. 105.

[25] *Contra Faustum,* XX, 21, *MPL,* XLII, 384—"Which Bishop, standing at the altar in the place of the saints' bodies, has ever said, 'We offer (sacrifice) to you, Peter, or Paul, or Cyprian'? Whatever is offered, is offered to God who has exalted the martyrs,—so that by recollection of

In those early days of the Faith, there was no such thing as an explicit science of Canon Law, distinct from Moral or Dogmatic theology. The Fathers and the bishops in their sermons and writings had primarily in mind the dogmatic aspects of the cult of relics, but hand-in-hand with their dogmatic justifications for the legitimacy and the value of the cult there was presented a canonical discipline to be observed. When St. Jerome was condemning an abuse, and St. Augustine explaining away a difficulty, they were holding up to the bishops and the people the right method of veneration. Their words were primarily and mainly dogmatic, but they were canonical as well, since they reflected the mind and the discipline of the early Church and Her bishops. It is from their words, therefore, that the canonical status of the cult in the first days may be learned. So far as is known today, there was no complete uniformity in the particular devotional practises except in the one most important particular that relics were not adored, but only venerated. On this point, there was complete uniform accord and unanimity.

Not only were there misunderstandings of the pagans to combat, but there were also internal abuses of the Christian people to stamp out. It would be strange if a devotion such as this, based on fervent affection for some saint of God or martyr to the Faith, could dawn in the Church without some abuses by credulous souls attending it. Love is ruled by the emotions, and the heart has its own laws and tendencies, distinct from the natural laws of reason and logic. St. Augustine alluded to some abuses in his writings, and severely criticized the monks who

---

those places a greater impulse arises to sharpen our love for those whom we imitate. We honor the martyrs, therefore, with the cult of love and association [societatis] that holy men in this life are honored, . . . but the former (martyrs) much more devotedly and surely, because of their conquest over trials." Cf. also *De Civitate Dei,* XXI, 8, *MPL,* XLI, 722—"We do not erect altars at these monuments that we may sacrifice to the martyrs, but to the one God of the martyrs and ourselves; and in this sacrifice they are named in their own place and rank as men of God who conquered the world by confessing Him, but they are not invoked by the sacrificing priest. For it is to God, not to them, that he sacrifices, though he sacrifices at their monument,—because he is God's priest, not theirs."

wandered through the lands selling relics for profit.[26] All this, of course, took place before the fifth century. The names of many people who trafficed in relics have come down in writing from past ages. A deacon, Deusdona by name, seems to have been the most unscrupulous in transactions, for he capitalized the desires for relics among the French and German people by ransacking the cemetery of Sts. Peter and Marcellinus, and selling their relics in the lands beyond the Alps.[27]

Neither the Church nor the Fathers of the Church were idle in this necessity. Imprudent piety and sentimentality could not be allowed free scope for their enthusiasm. Customs of erecting altars on the spots where the martyrs had fallen became so general that there were altars everywhere.[28] Local traditions had grown around these places many times, and it was found that in the course of time, many exaggerated claims were put forth in their favor. In the year 401, the fifth Council of Carthage passed the law that all such altars having no relics or corpus therein were to be demolished by the bishops.[29] If this could not be done, the bishops were to inform the people that they were to stay away from such places where it was so easy to foster superstition. Altars that had been erected on account of the inane private revelations or 'miraculous dreams' of some persons were to be destroyed. The Church was conscious of strict obligations

---

[26] *De Opere Monachorum,* XXVIII, 36, *MPL,* XL, 575; Bellarmine, *op. cit.,* II, 464; Thiers, *Traité des Superstitions,* tom. I, lib. 4, c. 4. In the text of St. Augustine, it is stated by the saint that monks ". . . circumferre et venditare membra martyrum, si tamen martyrum. . . ." He insinuated that there were grave doubts as to the authenticity of such relics carried about by private individuals. Bellarmine, in his text, answers objections raised from the text of St. Augustine by adversaries who wished to cast suspicion on the authenticity of all relics, whether honored in private cult, or by public cult in the churches.

[27] Marucchi, *Eléments d'archéologie chrétienne, transl.,* I, 104; Giraud, *"Le Commerce des Reliques,"* in *Mélanges G. B. de Rossi* (1892).

[28] There were different names for these memorial shrines to the saints. An altar erected anywhere in memory of the saint was called a *memoria;* if erected where the saint was buried, it was called a *sepulchrum;* if erected in the place where the saint was killed, it was a *martyrium;* if erected in the place where the saint had professed his faith in Christ, it was called a *confessio.* Cf. Gihr, *The Mass,* p. 236; Martigny, *Dict. Antiq. Chrét.,* p. 692.

[29] Mansi, III, 971.

and duties, and consequently was legislating for the canonical discipline of the faithful. This Council at Carthage presented the first positive criterion for determining the authenticity of relics: a long-standing and trustworthy tradition. It was the most logical and reasonable test to apply, because in past times, when there were no rules demanding that relics had to be approved in writing, the only means of finding the truth of a relic was to examine its history, and see whether devotion to it had been constant and non-interrupted. Once this was established as certainly existing, all presumptions of fact and of law favored conclusions that the relic was genuine.

The existence of a cult to relics from the fourth century is admitted by everyone. Even when the Nestorians and the Eutychians left the Faith in the fifth century, they did not reject the cult of relics, although they did reject other dogmas of the Church.[30]

Belief in the miraculous power of relics was common in those early days, and this led to many exaggerated acts of devotion to them. Some people began to sleep near the relics of the martyrs, thinking that proximity would bring them some grace and help.[31] Pope Damasus (366-384) steadied the right veneration, by writing many beautiful poems and verses to show that it was not mere proximity to relics which would bring virtue, but rather imitation of the virtues which made men saints.[32] Saint Augustine said the same in other words.[33]

Beautiful reliquaries were made for the relics, arranged in silver or gold or silk.[34] St. Chrysostom said that in his days the tombs of the martyrs were so magnificent that he would not

---

[30] Assemani, *Bibliotheca Orientalium,* IV, 7, 18.

[31] Marucchi, *Evidence of the Catacombs,* p. 65; *Dict. Apolog., art. cit.,* col. 916; Delehaye, *Legends of the Saints,* p. 169.

[32] "Hic congesta jacet quaeris se turba Piorum
Corpora sanctorum retinent veneranda sepulchra, . . .
Hic positus longa vixit qui in pace Sacerdos,
Hic confessores sancti, quos Graecia misit; . . .
Hic fateor Damasus volui mea condere membra,
Sed cineres timui sanctos vexare piorum."
—Pope Damasus, *Carmen* 34—*MPL,* XIII, 408.

[33] *De Cura pro Mortuis, MPL,* XL, 591-610.

[34] Prudentius, *Hymnus 3, ad S. Eulaliam, MPL,* LX, 355.

hesitate to prefer them to the palaces of the princes of the nation.[35]

In the sixth century, after Pope Gregory the Great had heard about the success of St. Augustine in England, he wrote and told the saint not to destroy the churches of the converted pagans, but rather ". . . to destroy only the idols, . . . and sprinkle the temples with holy water, build altars and put relics into them, . . . then use for Christian rites."[36] This is another strong indication that even though the West was presumed to be strict with reference to the dividing of relics, it was not so rigid or strict when it came to the question of finding relics for the altars of Eucharistic sacrifice. The Pontifical of Egbert, used in the consecration of churches in England, ". . . is replete with the most exquisite prayers . . ." for placing relics in altars.[37] The night-vigil of the people over the relics in the churchyard, the morning procession that carried the relics around the church three times, and finally the placing of the relics under the altar-slabs are all outlined with beauty and splendor in this Pontifical of the old Church in England.

By the end of the seventh century, the cult of relics was known all through the West, from Spain to Rome. All this time, the association of relics with the altars for the Sacrifice had been very intimate. When Pope Pascal I in the year 625 put relics of a martyr under the altars in Rome ". . . with his own hands . . ." he was only living up to the tradition of the past, and carrying on a custom existing since the second century.[38] The law of the second Council of Nicea, in the year 787, ruled that every consecration of churches had to be accompanied by the placing of relics in altars.[39] The law was strict, and it stated that bishops who consecrated altars without relics were to be deposed. But in spite of this, the Council of Chelsea in England, about thirty years later (in 816) mitigated the severity

---

[35] *Homil. 26, in Epist. 2 ad Corinth.,—MPG,* LXI, 582: "Sepulchra martyrum superant regias aulas. . . ."

[36] Bede, *Hist. Eccl.,* I, 29, and II, 159-161.

[37] Bridgett, *History of the Holy Eucharist in Great Britain,* p. 191; *Dict. Apolog. de la Foi Cath.,* IV, 912 and 916.

[38] *Regesta Romanorum Pontificum,* I, 50, and also pp. 40, 49, 51.

[39] Mansi, XIII, 751—in title 7.

of this former law. Here it was ruled that relics were to be used in the consecration of altars, but that if no relics were to be had, the Blessed Sacrament could be used instead.[40] Some altars were consecrated with the placing of a consecrated Host in the cavity intended for relics. Reiffenstuel mentions some old Missals which direct the priest-celebrant of Holy Mass to omit the prayer *"Oramus te, Domine, . . . quorum reliquiae hic sunt,"* in case that there are no relics in the altar.[41] The Roman Pontifical of the year 1596 made it a general law that all altars must have relics beneath the stone-table.

The Constitutions of Charlemagne stated that all oaths were to be pronounced either in a church, or over some relics.[42] At the Council of Compiegne, in 758, Tassilon swore allegiance to Pepin over the relics of martyrs.[43]

Devotion to the martyrs developed into keen rivalry, and it was not uncommon that different localities bent all their efforts to acquire the relics of their favorite saints. Demand created a supply, and just as long as there was a demand for relics, so long also were there men unscrupulous enough to furnish a supply to meet it. Thurston has some worth while comment on this:

> What was in the long run hardly less disastrous than fraud or avarice was the keen rivalry between religious centres, and the eager credulity fostered by the desire to be known as the possessors of some unusually startling relic. We learn from Cassian in the fifth century that there were monks who seized upon certain martyrs' bodies by force of arms, defying the authority of the bishops, and this was a story which we find many times repeated in the Western chronicles of a later date.
>
> In such an atmosphere of lawlessness, doubtful relics came to abound. . . . There is no reason for supposing in most cases the existence of deliberate fraud. . .[44]

---

[40] Hardouin, *Acta Conciliorum,* IV, 1220; Thurston, "Relics," *Cath. Encycl.,* XII, 737; Bliley, Altars, p. 39.

[41] *Jus Canonicum,* lib. III, tit. XL, n. 40.

[42] Mansi, XIII, 1102—the formula contained ". . . et ista patrocinia Sanctorum. . . ." Cf. also Mansi, XIII, 1066—"Ut omne sacramentum [i.e., oath] juretur in Ecclesia aut supra reliquias."

[43] *Dict. Prat. des Connaiss. Relig.,* V, 1180.

[44] Thurston, "Relics," *Cath. Encycl.,* XII, 737.

St. Augustine had railed against the abuses in his own day, but what he saw in the fourth century was as nothing compared with what he could have seen in later days. Some have said that it was an age in which faith was supreme, superstition rampant, and historical criticism nil. Judging by the standards of this present day, it was an age totally uncritical and strangely morbid in its devotions. No relic was too fantastic or bizarre. Good faith, in its ignorance, saw the hand of God making all things first of all possible, then probable, and finally actual. There are many cases where it is possible to prove that relics were duplicated, both by well-meaning people and by knaves. The mere probability that some bone was the relic of a martyr too often passed over into a firm conviction that it was an actual relic.[45] Nails that had touched the Nails of the True Cross, and wood that had been touched to the wood of the Cross, became in many instances reputed relics of the original. This does not show any fault in the law; it merely accentuates some foible of human nature.[46]

ART. 2. ROMAN LAW ON RELICS

It was a law of ancient Rome that persons who had been condemned to death were not to be allowed the privilege of burial according to the Roman customs.[47] This law, seemingly so strict, was modified and softened by another law which ruled that the body of such a dead person could be handed over to the relatives or the friends, if they should ask for it. This latter law is in the Digests of Justinian, 48:24:1, 2 and 3.

---

[45] Delehaye, *Legends of the Saints,* p. 170; Mioni, *Il Culto delle Reliq.,* cap. 4; Honoratus a S. Maria, *Regulae Critices,* V, 427 and 453.

[46] Cf. *Analecta Bollandiana,* XIX (1900), 46 seq. In this place is told an incident of a learned man of past centuries who was more ready to admit a miracle than face an apparently obvious fact. Confronted with two heads of the same saint, he readily professed that God had worked a miracle of duplication. The author of the article classifies this attitude as typical of the general feeling up to the late Middle Ages, i.e., from the ninth to the fifteenth centuries.

[47] Mommsen, *La Droit Pénal Romain,* I, 338; Northcote, *Roma Sotteranea,* p. 56. Burial according to the Roman laws made the place of interment a *locus sacer,* exempt from taxes, incapable of suffering prescription, and the recipient of other special privileges.

> 48:24:1—(Ulpian). The bodies of those who have been condemned to death are not to be denied to their relatives. This rule was followed even by Divus Augustus, in his Life. . . . The bodies of those who have been burned to death may be asked from the magistrates, in order that their ashes or their cinders may be collected and buried.
> 48:24:3—(Paulus). The bodies of those punished are to be given to anyone who petitions for them.

When the Empire became Christian, in the first part of the fourth century, there were no explicit laws against the possession of relics, although there were other laws which insisted upon the inviolability of tombs, in accord with the traditional reverence of the Romans for the places of the dead.[48] In the year 386, however, the cult of relics had reached such proportions among the Christian people that public policy had to be formed so as to prevent widespread buying and selling. Accordingly, the Emperors Gratian, Theodosius and Valentinian passed a law which forbade the sale or the transfer of any martyr's body or relics. This law is in the Theodosian Code IX, xvii, 7:

> Let no one transfer an interred body to another place: let no one divide a martyr's body: let no body be sold.

In 432 it was reaffirmed by different emperors, probably for the same reasons as formerly.[49] It also found its way into the Code of Justinian.

> *Code,* 1:2:2—*On the place of the Apostles and Martyrs.* Let no one think that the tombs of the Apostles or Martyrs is allowed for [the burial-place of] human bodies.
> *Code,* 1:2:3—*On the Relics of Martyrs.* Let no one divide (distrahat) martyrs: no one is to be sold.

Brunnemann comments on this latter title, and says that anyone who acted contrary to that law did nothing validly. All contracts of purchase or sale made over a relic were invalid, and the guilty persons were punishable by a severe penalty.[50] An earlier law, made by Antoninus and Balbinus, in the year 214, also was embodied into the Justinian Code, but although it is titled *"On the Translation of Relics,"*

---

[48] Digests 47:12 and Code 9:19 both are titled *"De Sepulchro Violato."*
[49] *Codex Theod.,* IX, xlv, 5, 8.
[50] Brunnemann, *Commentarium in Quinquaginta libros Pandectarum* (Coloniae Allobrogum), I, 5.

it refers rather to the ordinary transfers of human bodies such as are necessary in every community at different times and occasions.[51] The last law in this title, however, was a repetition of an earlier law of 386, and it stated:

> Let no one transfer an interred body to another place without the consent (sine affatibus) of Augustus.[52]

These laws were all intended to correct abuses which had been prevalent, and, to some extent, they accomplished their purpose. They were not wholly successful, however, and that for several reasons. In the first place, there was a tremendous difference between the cult of relics in the East and in the West. In the West, the people obeyed the laws, for the most part, but in the East the laws were almost totally disregarded.[53] It was in the East that the habit of opening the tombs and distributing the relics originated, and this custom did not become common in Rome until the end of the seventh century.[54] The civil law in the West was protected not only by statute but by custom as well, so that even the Empress Constantina could not break through it. When she wrote to Pope Gregory in 593, asking for the head of Saint Paul, in order that she might add glory and renown to her new chapel in the imperial palace, the Pope absolutely refused to grant her request. The words of his refusal show clearly and positively that he was not in favor of the extremes that the East was in the habit of reaching, even though they possessed real relics of real Saints.[55] He did send to her, however, some secondary relics, such as veils and cloths which had touched the tombs of the Apostles.[56]

---

[51] *Code,* 3:44—*De Translatione Reliquiarum.*

[52] Code, 3:44:14.

[53] Wernz, *Jus Decretalium,* III, 384; *Dict. Apolog. de la Foi Cath.,* IV, 911; Thurston, "Relics," *Cath. Encycl.,* XII, 736,—where this last point is well treated. Honoratus a S. Maria, *Animadversiones,* V, 453, also writes of the abuses which the Roman law intended to correct.

[54] Some authors assign an earlier date than this, but others maintain that it was later. Probably when the Catacombs were sacked in the seventh century, or thereabouts, the general use and ownership of relics was common in the West as well as in the East.

[55] *Registrum Epistolarum Gregorii I Papae,* IV, 30—*MGH,* I, 264-266.

[56] These were called *brandea,* and were common throughout the West. Sometimes they were made to resemble the genuine relic, so that they would be an image of the original thing. Honoratus a S. Maria lists many

But even in the West, the law against the taking or removing of relics was not too strictly enforced. Religious practises were quietly tolerated, though they ran counter to the strict letter of the laws against the handling of relics or their removal. As late as the year 459, the emperors Leo and Julian enacted another law to the effect that relics of the Saints had to be kept in a church, and were not to be allowed to ornament profane places. The place where they were to be kept was at the discretion of the bishops.[57] There were actual translations of relics from the East into the West, without any open disapproval from the civil law. The body of St. Dionysius was sent from the East to Milan and a letter of St. Basil to St. Ambrose shows that there was no secrecy about the translation in any way. St. Basil said that his people did not want to part with the relics, but that they had finally consented for religious motives. "Princes and powers could not have forced them to part with the relics. . . . They are as sorrowful to part with them, as you are glad to receive them. Your joy is their consolation." [58]

The law's divergencies seem to have been based on the two purposes of ending the abuses and at the same time allowing due and fit reverence to the Saints.[59]

ART. 3. EARLY ATTEMPTS TO DETERMINE AUTHENTICITY

Century-old or immemorial traditions, against which nothing has ever been preached or taught, are solid facts, capable of producing complete moral certainty. In such traditions, there is not only the *maxima probabilitas* found in strong presumptions, but there is also the element of stability and unswerving steadfastness of devotion which amounts to the certain conclu-

---

such *brandea,* and shows how in the course of time many of them were mistakenly thought to be the authentic relic. Such were imitation nails of the Passion and Cross of Christ, replicas of the veil of the Virgin Mary, copies of the chains of Saints Peter and Paul. Cf. *Animadversiones,* V, 459-464, and Zallwein, *Principia,* II, 144.

[57] *Code,* 1:3:26—"Decernimus. . . ."

[58] St. Basil, Epist. CXCVII—*MPG,* XXXII, 710-714.

[59] De Rossi, *La Roma Sotterranea Cristiana,* II, 73-80, mentions translations of relics which were not prevented by the civil laws of Rome. When the motive was purely religious the law did not forbid the honor to relics.

sion that the veneration which is now correct began in the right way, with a true relic as its foundation.[60]

The fifth Council of Carthage, in 401, gave official recognition to this means of verifying relics by accepting as authentic those which were substantiated by the testimony in a long-standing and trustworthy tradition.[61] The Council did not go on record as maintaining that any tradition proved the relics to be authentic, because its main purpose in this canon was to decree the legitimate places of public prayer, and not the setting-up of rules for the verification of relics. In fulfilling its main purpose, however, it adopted the rule of accepting long traditions as having proving power.

The attitude of the early Church, in supervising not merely the relics in public cult but those in private use as well, may be seen from the condemnation of Lucilla, a Donatist, by Cecilian, the archbishop of Carthage. He rebuked her for kissing a relic that was not authenticated, as preparation for receiving the Holy Eucharist. Not only was her devotion unbalanced and misplaced, but it was misguided as well, because of her veneration for a thing which was not surely a relic of the saints.[62]

The ritual-forms for the primitive (and now obsolete) trials by fire, or the ordeals, established in order to ascertain whether relics were true or fictitious, are still extant, and these tests for determining the authenticity date back to the sixth century, at least.[63] This ancient rite was not done privately

---

[60] Mabillon, *Lettre d'une Benedictin à M. l'Eveque de Blois, touchant le discernement des anciennes reliques, au sujet d'une dissertation de M. Thiers contre le sainte Larme de Vendôme.* The whole trend of this work is the development of such proofs, drawn from antiquity of devotions.

[61] Mansi, III, 971 ". . . in fidelissima traditione. . . ."

[62] Optatus Milevitanus, *De Schismate Donatistarum,* I, 16, *MPL,* XI, 917.

[63] Mabillon, *Vetera Analecta,* p. 569. In *Acta Ss. Ordinis Bened.,* III, 658, the same author tells of a trial by fire which vindicated the truth of the relics, because they were not consumed by the flames after they had been thrown therein during the Canon of the Mass. Wernz, *Jus Decret.,* III, 384, takes issue with Hefele, *Histoire des Conciles,* III, 57, on the translation of words in canon 2, of the Council of Caesaraugustus (592). The words are: ". . . Igne comburentur reliquiae inventae. . . ." Hefele says that the priests are told to destroy these newly-found relics by burning them, but Wernz says that these words command priests to have an *experimentum ignis,* or a trial by fire. Wernz seems to quote better proof for his contention than Hefele, because he relies on a better manuscript

either, but with a solemn formula of prayers and actions. This service consisted of the chanting of eleven psalms, followed by a long prayer. At the end of this, the *Pater Noster* was recited, with an antiphon and psalm. During this last psalm, the relics on trial were placed in the middle of the fire. "Sicque faciens, Reliquiae utrum verae sint an falsae, reperies." The prayer used in this ceremony was beautiful, for it showed the anxiety of the Church in her endeavors to have a pure and worthy cult.

> Oremus. Domine Deus, Jesu Christe, qui es Rex regum et Dominus dominantium, et amator omnium in te credentium, qui es justus judex, fortis et prudens; qui sacerdotibus tuis tua sancta mysteria revelasti, et qui tribus Pueris flammis ignium mitigasti: concede nobis indignis famulis tuis, et exaudi preces nostras, ut pannus iste vel filum istud quibus involuta sunt ista corpora Sanctorum, si vera non sunt, crementur ab hoc igne, et si vera sint, evadere valeant; ut justitiae non dominetur aequitas, subdatur falsitas veritati; quatenus veritas tua ibi declaretur, et nobis omnibus in te credentibus manifestetur, ut cognoscamus quia tu es Deus benedictus in saecula saeculorum. Amen.

St. Martin of Tours was probably the most zealous promoter of honor and veneration to relics in the young Church, but even he was not swept off his feet in the formation of devotional practises. Sulpicius Severus tells how St. Martin demolished the tomb of a supposed martyr, when he found that an error had been made, and that the body of another not a martyr was being honored by mistake.[64] Therefore, as early as the year 397 (the date of the Saint's death), it was common doctrine that devotion was allowed only to true and authentic relics.

Saint Augustine had demanded that a list be compiled, narrating all the cures and miracles wrought through the relics.[65] These lists were not intended primarily to establish the authenticity of the relics, but they would by their very nature tend to

---

edition of the Conciliar decrees. Nothing can establish certainty about the precise meaning of that canon of the Council, however, for no contemporary writings can be found to explain it. Zallwein, *Principia Juris Ecclesiastici*, II, 147, is convinced that it was a trial by fire.

[64] Sulpicius Severus, *De Vita Beati Martini*, xi—*MPL*, XX, 166-167; Zallwein, *Principia Juris Ecclesiastici, II*, 147.

[65] *De Civitate Dei*, XXII, 8—*MPL*, XLI, 760 ss.

protect them from suspicion. They are not in existence today, because of the ravages of time and war.[66]

ART. 4. CONCILIAR LEGISLATION, NUCLEUS FOR LATER LAWS

The great political upheavals of the Middle Ages had an effect upon relics of the saints. The invading Lombards had demolished many churches and shrines, and had stolen or destroyed many of the sacred remains interred therein. Pope Paul I ordered that all the bodies of the saints were to be taken within the walls of the churches of the city, so as to prevent their desecration by invaders.[67] In similar cases, relics had been carried away by monks, when they were being exiled from their monasteries. Pagan temples in the city of Rome became Christian churches, and the shrines for the remains of the saints. Thus did the pagan temple of the Pantheon become a Christian church, and received the new name *Sancta Maria ad Martyres* because of the multitude of relics which it contained. The cult of the one true God on the identical spot where previously there had been idols adored would expiate the sacrilege of former times.[68]

The first explicit law of the Church on the cult of relics came with the II Council of Nicea, in the year 787. This Council had the Iconoclasts as its main problem, and through all its decrees there runs the idea of preserving the traditions of the Fathers and of the past. It quoted the words of St. Paul to the Thessalonians (II Epistle, ii, 14) "Therefore, brethren, stand fast: hold to the traditions which you have learned, whether by word or by our epistle," and defended the use of images in the churches, partly by appealing to the past customs and traditions. The Council took the position that whosoever honored an image, honored the person whose image it was, because the honor and reverence passed through the thing to the person represented by it.[69] The Council went on to say the same about

[66] D'Alès, "Martyre," *Dict. Apol. de la Foi Cath.*, III, 372.

[67] Marucchi, *Elements d'archeologie Chretienne*, I, 102-104; Northcote, *Roman Catacombs*, p. 67; *Dict. Apol. de la Foi Cath.*, IV 916.

[68] Perrone, *Praelectiones Theologicae*, II, 433, n. 4; Delehaye, *Legends of the Saints*, p. 171 seq.

[69] "Imaginis honor ad primitivum transit, et qui adorat imaginem, adorat

relics, stating that ". . . whoever dares to cast out the sacred relics of martyrs, . . . or to undermine the legitimate traditions of the Catholic Church is to be punished. If they are bishops or clerics, they are to be deposed; if they are monks or layfolk, they are to be excommunicated.[70]

Saint John Damascene, the strenuous opponent of Iconoclasm in all its forms, also defended the cult of relics, and his words of defense gave not only a dogmatic explanation of the devotion, but at the same time some implied canonical rules for the discipline to be followed in the acts of veneration.[71] His words are so noteworthy that the Church has made them the three lessons for the second nocturne, on the Feast of Holy Relics.

In the year 813, the first Council of Mayence, in canon 51, made the law that no one had the right to transfer relics from one place to another without permission.[72] Gratian took this regulation into his Decretum.[73] Then came the IV Lateran Council in the year 1215, under the famous Pope Innocent III, ruling that no relics were to be exposed for veneration unless they were placed in a fit container or reliquary.[74] The Decretals of Gregory IX adopted the same law, almost word for word, and took away from the Bishops the right of approving newly-found saints' relics. Henceforth, such approbations had to come from the Roman Pontiff.[75] Heretofore, every bishop had been the absolute judge in his diocese, but after the Council of the Lateran and the Decretals of Gregory IX, the jurisdiction in the authentication of newly discovered relics was reserved to the Holy See.

At the same time there were constitutions of bishops in Eng-

---

in ea depicti imaginem." Cavallera, *Thesaurus Doctrinae Catholicae*, p. 445, n. 828.

[70] Mansi, XIII, 751; Denziger, *Enchiridion Symbolorum*, p. 104 seq.

[71] *De Fide Orthodoxa*, IV, 15—*MPG*, XCIV, 1163-1166—*Quis sanctis ipsorumque reliquiis habendus sit.*

[72] Labbe, *Concilia*, VII, 1253; Hardouin, *Coll. Conc.*, IV, 1007; Sirmond, *Conc. Gall.*, IV, 2737; Hefele, *Histoire des Conc.*, IIIb, 1142.

[73] C. 37, D. I, *de consecratione*.

[74] "Ne reliquiae Ss. ostendantur extra capsum: ne novae habeantur in veneratione sine Romana Ecclesia."—Tit. 62, Mansi, XXII, 1050.

[75] Cf. c. 2, X, *de reliquiis et veneratione sanctorum*, III, 45. Cf. also c. 1, *de reliquiis et veneratione Ss.*, III, 22, in VI°; c. 1, *de reliq. et vener. Ss.*, III, 16 in Clem., c. 1, *de reliq. et vener. Ss.*, III, 12 in Extray. Commun.

land under Stephen Langton, ruling that all altars must be equipped with the proper appurtenances. These laws presupposed that there were relics in all the altar-stones, as was expressly stated.[76]

The General Council of Lyons, in the year 1274, passed a law which had for its purpose the obtaining of documents proving the authenticity of relics used in public cult. This law of the Council of Lyons was probably the first and the earliest general legislation demanding that all relics be authenticated in writing.[77] St. Augustine had demanded this centuries before,[78] but his idea was not so much to authenticate the truth of the relic as to keep an account of the number and the nature of miracles worked through the relics.[79] It was not until 1274, however, that written authentication became commanded by law in a general Council. England knew about this law, because thirteen years later the Bishop of Exeter quoted it, and demanded that it be observed in his diocese.[80]

St. Thomas Aquinas treated the question of relics in his *Summa,* and gave the Scholastic view on the legitimacy and the nature of the cult.[81] In his usual manner, the Angelic Doctor, first of all proposed objections against his thesis, then stated the dogma of the Church, and proceeded finally to answer the objections. In his explanation of the law of the Church, he says:

> As Augustine says (De Civitate Dei, i): "If a father's coat or ring, or anything else of that kind, is so much more cherished by his children as love for one's parents is greater, in no way are the bodies themselves to be despised, which

---

[76] Mansi, XXXIa, 424.

[77] Cf. "Reliques," *Dict. Pratique,* V, 1179; Mioni, *Il Culto delle Relique,* cap. 10.

[78] *De Civitate Dei,* XXII, 8—*MPL,* XLI, 760.

[79] Delehaye, *Les Origines de Culte,* p. 149 seq. These lists, or *libelli,* ordered by St. Augustine are not extant today; most probably they have perished with the lapse of time. They were an initial effort to establish objective truth, uncolored by any personal attitudes, favorable or unfavorable. They were intended to be read aloud to the people assembled in church, as a proof of God's power and Providence working through the relics of saints. Cf. "Martyre," *Dict. Apolog.,* III, 372.

[80] Cf. "Reliques," *Dict. Pratique,* V, 1179; Thurston, "Relics," *Cath. Encycl.,* XII, 737.

[81] *Summa Theologica,* III, Q. 25, a. 6.

are more intimately united to us than any garment; for they belong to man's very nature." It is clear from this that he who has a certain affection for anyone, venerates whatever is left after his death, not only his body and the parts thereof, but even external things, such as his clothes and such-like. Now it is manifest that we should show honor to the saints of God, as being members of Christ, the children and friends of God, and our intercessors. Wherefore, in memory of them we ought to honour any relic of theirs in a fitting manner: principally their bodies, which were temples, and organs of the Holy Ghost dwelling and operating in them, and are destined to be likened to the Body of Christ by the glory of the Resurrection. Hence God Himself fittingly honors such relics by working miracles at their presence. . . . We do not worship an insensible body for its own sake, but for the sake of the soul, which was once united thereto, and now enjoys God. . . . The dead body of a saint is not identical with that which the saint had during life, on account of the difference in form—viz, the soul: but it is the same by identity of matter, which is destined to be reunited to its form.[82]

From this time on (after the thirteenth century) there was a steady stream of canonical rules for the liturgical use and veneration of relics. The diocese most affected by the abuses ensured a right observance by salutary laws which both curbed the excesses and extremes, and furthered the true devotion. In the heart of the territory which is now France, relics had been honored from early centuries. Consequently, the provincial and diocesan synods in that territory were better able to know the cult and legislate upon it than were the synods in other places not so situated.

In or about the year 1300, there were two diocesan synods, one at Constance,[83] and the other at Bayeux.[84] These repeated for their own subjects the same essential law as that of the Council of the Lateran in 1215. The synod of Constance, however, added a sanction to its law by declaring that the Bishop had the right to excommunicate anyone who made out of relics a means to

[82] *The "Summa Theologica" of St. Thomas Aquinas,* translation by the Fathers of the English Dominican Province, New York, 1913.

[83] Mansi, XXV, 34.

[84] Mansi, XXV, 62.

acquire gain or profit in money matters. Besides, lay-folk were forbidden to carry relics, or to take them from the churches. These were efficient methods of killing abuses. The canonical rules were growing in number and importance.

In 1311, the II Council of Ravenna,[85] and in 1326, the Council of Marciace,[86] both devoted titles to the use and the care of relics. This was done to ". . . reform discipline and morals . . ." as the Council at Ravenna declared. The legislation is interesting in these Councils because of the demands that all relics be authenticated before they are to be used in public devotion. The law of the Council of Marciace ran thus:

> . . . So that relics of the Saints be more reverently venerated in the future, and lest Christian simplicity be deceived by figments and false documents . . . we command that hereafter ancient relics are not to be displayed outside their containers or reliquaries. Let no one presume to venerate relics newly-found, unless they have been approved by the Roman Church. Let no dealer [quaestor] be permitted to carry relics or cross or chain, or to preach about them in public churches, without these same letters of approbation,—unless the bishop grant special permission. . . .

The Council of Angers, in 1448, had particular reasons for wishing to eradicate abuses in the cult, because that territory had been overrun by persons who wished to make money through the sale of relics. Their canonical provisions were based on public decency as well as upon the respect due to the saints. "Because it is not right that relics of the saints be carted through the world for the sake of acquiring money, and because some people have carried them even through our own territory, the Council forbids that any relics be carried through the province for that purpose. The bishop is charged to stop this, should it happen again."[87]

All these provincial Councils and synods of central Europe and England furnished the incentive and the background for the law on relics in the Council of Trent. Protestantism had

---

[85] Tit. 5—Mansi, XXV, 453.
[86] Tit. 41—Mansi, XXV, 792.
[87] Mansi, XXXII, 91.

discarded and ridiculed the cult, terming relics "dead things which sanctify no one." [88]

The Fathers of the Tridentine Council took up the question in the 25th session, and went into the subject at some length in the title *"On the Invocation, Veneration, Relics and Sacred Images of the Saints."* They did not make a single new law; neither did they change any existing law. They merely reaffirmed and stated the rules and the legislation which the Church had held for centuries beforehand. The true reason and the legitimacy of the practise were defined and explained, just as the Fathers of the first three centuries had written.

> The sacred bodies of the martyrs and the others now living with Christ, who, when alive, were members of Christ and temples of the Holy Ghost . . . are to be venerated by the faithful, because through them God gives many benefits to men. . . . So that whoever asserts that veneration and honor are not due to the relics of the saints . . . is to be condemned absolutely. Just as the Church in the past acted in this matter, so now also in the present.
>
> Moreover, all superstition . . . in the matter of relics is to be completely stopped. All disgraceful traffic for profit is to be eliminated. All manner of acting which savors of extravagance is to be avoided. All abuses in the honor or the visitation of relics must cease. Bishops are charged to see to it that nothing unfitting . . . is to be allowed. New relics are not to be received for veneration unless with the approbation and the knowledge of the bishop. If the bishop is in doubt about any matter or any relic, he is not to settle any question without recourse to the Holy See through the proper channels . . .[89]

Following the Council of Trent, diocesan synods and Councils

---

[88] The principal writings of the Reformers against relics have been collected into one book, published at Geneva in 1599. It has four parts: the first is by Calvin, *"Traitté des Reliques"*; the other three are by unknown authors, and are titled thus: *"Autre Traitté des Reliques contre le Decret du Concile de Trente," "Inventaire des Reliques de Rome,"* and *"Response aux allégations de Robert Bellarmin Jésuite pour les Reliques."* Vollet, "Reliques," *La Grande Encyclopedie,* XXVIII, 367, and Hauck, "Relics," *The Jewish Encyclopedia,* XXIII, 59-62, agree with the Reformers on this matter.

[89] Conc. Trident., Sess. XXV, *De Invocation, Veneratione, et Reliquiis Sanctorum et Sacris Imaginibus* (on December 3rd and 4th, 1563). Cf. also Cavallera, *Thesaurus Doctrinae Catholicae,* p. 441, nn. 819-823.

were held more often, and these passed many statutes for the care of relics. The Council of Mayence, in 1549, encouraged the cult, but not the extremes to which it could be carried. "Relics are incentives to faith and encouragement, on account of the example of the saints." [90]

In 1565 came the law of the I Council of Milan, with its commands for diocesan reform and good order.[91] In title 30, bishops were told to make their visitations and to investigate ". . . whether the relics of the saints are preserved in places that are safe, honorable and decent." Title 9 of the same Council has general rules for the cult. They are practically the same as the regulations in the Council of Trent, and in fact, Bishops are told to obey the laws of the Council of Trent faithfully. Two years later, the Council of Sipontinum (probably Dordogne) passed the same regulations.[92] Later, in 1573, the Council of Florence stated that relics were not even to be touched, unless it were for the cause of devotion.[93] The punishment for the infraction of this law was at the discretion of the bishop.

The year 1576 saw two Councils, one at Naples,[94] and the other at Milan.[95] The rules set up by the Council of Naples were nothing more than a repetition of those in former councils, but those formulated at the Council of Milan mark what can rightly be called a semi-climax in the growth and liturgy on the cult of relics. Called into session by Charles Borromaeo, its purpose was reorganization and good administration in his ecclesiastical province. He passed the law that all relics in the province and all bodies of Saints were to be investigated, and this by specially delegated priests and religious, according to a plan set by himself. First, all letters, documents and charts concerning relics were to be examined diligently. Witnesses with a reputation for sanctity and good-esteem could be questioned in regard to their knowledge concerning the relics. When certitude had been acquired from these different testimonies, the

[90] Title 49—Mansi, XXXII, 1415.
[91] Mansi, XXXIVa, 44.
[92] Mansi, XXXV, 866.
[93] Mansi, XXXVa, 729.
[94] Mansi, XXXV, 807.
[95] Mansi, XXXIVa, 184-190 and 207.

bishops were to draw up a list of all the authentic relics, and this was to be preserved forever in the episcopal archives. Relics newly-found were to be recorded on that list. All those which were used in public devotions had to be approved by the local bishop, even though they belonged to exempt religious. No private person was to have them without special permission. The inscriptions and names on the graves or relics of Saints were to be clearly written and renewed whenever necessary. In addition to these regulations, there were many other detailed rules, for every ecclesiastical ceremony that centered about relics. The genius of St. Charles Borromaeo shines through all this relic-legislation, for it is the fountain-head of all the liturgy on the cult. Many of its statutes are still in the Code, untouched since that time. It anticipated by forty years the earliest decree concerning relics from the Congregation of Rites.

The council of Bourges, in 1584, devoted title 10 to relics.[96] A short prologue defended the practise and the cult by referring to the reply of St. Jerome to Vigilantius, and also to the story of the bones of Elias which brought back life to a dead man, as told in IV Kings, 13:21. Following the prologue are five short canons giving general regulations. Bishops were told to preach the devotion to their people, and lay-folk were again told that if they possessed any relics in their homes they were to bring them to the church and relinquish them. Even in processions, only the clergy were allowed to carry them, unless there was an ancient custom allowing lay people to participate and share that honor.

In 1585, there were two Councils of the Church legislating on relics, one at Aix and the other in Mexico. The same general rules and laws made by the other councils on the Continent were promulgated for the churches of Mexico as well.[97] At Aix, the Council reaffirmed the laws of Trent, as the others had done, and further added that the bishops must be ready to resist the clamors of the populace in regard to newly-found relics.[98] It is not possible to ascertain with certitude the precise motive

---

[96] Mansi, XXXIVa, 888.
[97] Mansi, XXXIVb, 1135.
[98] Mansi, XXXIVb, 997.

which caused this last rule to be inserted in the conciliar decrees. Probably there was a recurrence of old abuses, when relics of doubtful authenticity were hailed by popular esteem as true and certain. In the supervision of such suspicious relics, the bishops were told to have no regard for the erroneous popular beliefs, once that the relics were known to be false. This centralization of power in the bishops, giving them the right to approve and supervise relics for their own diocese, without having recourse to Rome, began in the laws of the Council of Trent, and is still in force. In exceptional cases, of course, the Roman Pontiff was to be consulted, as the Council of Aix clearly stated.

A new trend in the law in France, and also a gratifying one, owing to the conditions of the times, came with the law of the Council of Avignon in 1594.[99] In that locality at the time, there were many heretics abusing the Church, and there was a real necessity for strict laws, both for offense and defense. After the Council had legislated on the general observances of the cult, it told each bishop to promulgate the law ". . . that whoever takes, receives, or steals relics is excommunicated *latae sententiae*." This tendency to protect relics from all manner of desecration increased, until the year 1613, when Pope Paul V declared that excommunication *latae sententiae* reserved to the Roman Pontiff was incurred by anyone who took minute or even fragmentary relics of the Saints from the Roman Catacombs.[100]

The same law was repeated by Clement X, in the constitution "*Ex Commissae*" on January 13, 1672. This decree of the Pope is important, because it shows what was the attitude of the Roman See, in all doubts and anxieties over the verity or the legitimacy of relics. Special permission had to be obtained to take away relics from the Roman Catacombs, and that permission could be obtained only from the Cardinal Vicar of the city, acting in the name of the Holy Father. It was necessary to have written permission, and besides, the presence of a spe-

[99] Mansi, XXXIVb, 1344.

[100] Avanzini, *De Constitutione Apostolicae Sedis*, p. 102; Ballerini-Palmieri, *Opus Theol. Morale*, VII, 262; Bucceroni, *Institut. Theol. Moral.*, II, 512; Lehmkuhl, *Theol. Mor.*, II, 710; Leech, *Comparative Study*, p. 70; Paul V, decrees of August 24, 1613, and May 16, 1614.

cially delegated priest was required at the actual moment of disinterring the relics. The decree of the Pope runs thus:

> *Ad futuram rei memoriam.* Because of the sacred pastoral duty committed to us from above, we, wishing to take care that the bodies of martyrs and their relics will be piously, without money-traffic, and with decency removed from the cemeteries of our city and adjacent places, and protected, guarded and preserved with prudence and fitness, took the experienced counsel and the serious advice of selected officials in the Roman Curia and other prelates. At our command, they gave this question mature deliberation, and their decision was carried to us by our beloved son, Cardinal Gaspar (Carpineus) Vicar General of the City, and our Prodatarius. By Apostolic authority and by these present letters, we prescribe and command that no person is to take relics from these aforesaid cemeteries, unless with written permission, signed and sealed by Cardinal Gaspar, or the acting Vicar General of the city.
>
> Nor is anyone, under pain of excommunication *latae sententiae,* to disinter bones or any body, nor to take the like from any such cemetery unless before a priest delegated by Cardinal Gaspar, or whoever happens to be Vicar General of the city. This priest is to investigate and identify, diligently and exactly, the place, the inscriptions, and the signs of martyrdom which the Congregation of our brother Cardinals for the care of Indulgences and Relics has decided as certain marks of recognition.
>
> When the identification has been completed, the bodies and the relics must be put immediately into separate caskets or containers that are closed with a seal. They must be taken then to the city, to be placed in our palace and guarded by our venerable brother Joseph Eusavius, at present the bishop of Helenopolitanus and also Papal Sacristan, or by any other priest of sound reputation designated by Cardinal Gaspar or the Cardinal Vicar.
>
> These bodies and relics are not to be distributed or publicly exposed to cult and veneration before they are examined by the Cardinal Vicar, and approved by the authority of the Roman Pontiff or the aforesaid Congregation of Cardinals.
>
> Because it is right that sacred bodies and relics which are notable (*insignes*) namely, the head, leg or that part of the body in which the martyr suffered—if it be entire—should not be kept by lay-folk or in private houses, but in a church, we command that in the future these relics be given to no

person who does not bring letters from his Ordinary. The Cardinal Vicar will learn from these letters about the dignity of the church which asks for the relics, the fitness of granting the request, and the assurance that in the future these relics will be preserved and cherished in their proper religious setting.

Exempted from this rule are both the great princes and the leading Church prelates, toward whom we wish to be more liberal; and lest the rest of the faithful be deprived of such sacred things, we allow that lesser relics (*minus insignes*) be given to them.

Always there must be moderation observed, lest the abundance of sacred things cause a loss of esteem for them. This must be carefully avoided. In addition to this, a book is to be kept in which are noted the bodies and the relics extracted from these cemeteries, together with the names of the persons and the churches to whom they have been distributed. Moreover, the persons who decorate or sell the reliquaries and the caskets in which the relics are deposited are not to assign any new names, other than those already imposed by Cardinal Gaspar or the Cardinal Vicar, under penalty of a fine of twenty-five *scuti monetae* or other punitive sanctions determined by the Cardinal Vicar. In order that all occasions of mercenary traffic be removed, the Cardinal Vicar may use the money donated for pious causes, in order to pay those persons whose labor was required for disinterring and extracting the sacred bodies. The Cardinal Vicar will determine the right amount for their expenses and payment.

Finally we severely forbid, under penalty of immediate excommunication *latae sententiae*, that any emolument however small be received under any pretext—even though freely offered—in the handling of the bodies and the relics, or in the writing of their sealed and signed documentations.

All other laws to the contrary not being valid against this letter. . . . Given at Rome, at St. Mary Major's, under the seal of the Fisherman, on January 13, 1672, in the second year of our Pontificate.[101]

That this was the set policy in regard to the transfer of relics is known as certain from a letter of Benedict XIV, on March 5, 1742, when the same provisions and regulations were set down.[102] At that time, the *promoter fidei* was given the right to transfer

[101] *Bullarium Romanum,* XVIII, 296.

[102] *Bullarium Romanum Benedicti* XIV, I, const. 46, p. 154.

the body of Venerable Camillus de Lellis to a better location, but at the same time many detailed instructions were set down. Only certain persons could go into the crypt, others being forbidden under penalty of an excommunication *latae sententiae* reserved to the Holy Father. Those who did enter the crypt were told to investigate most carefully (accuratissime) each and every object therein which would testify to the authenticity of the body. They were forbidden under pain of excommunication *latae sententiae* and other penalties and censures [103] to take the least part or the smallest relic of the body. When the body had been identified, it was to be placed in some safe receptacle that could be fastened and sealed with wax. All the necessary faculties were given to the investigators to retain the body in their custody until further notice, when some set location would be assigned to it. The decree was signed by Passioneus, then Cardinal Vicar of Rome. The whole process is the same as that set up by Clement X, seventy years before.

But even before the close of the sixteenth century, many other laws on relic-legislation had been printed and sent forth. The Roman Pontifical had been printed in 1596, under Clement VIII, and this settled many disputes and doubts by demanding that relics be placed in all altars, under penalty of invalid consecration if they were not used and deposited therein.[104] In the same year (1596) the Council of Salerno, in canon 6, restated the Tridentine law for its territory.[105] Before the close of the century, a Council at Amalphi devoted four canons to the matter of relics, and passed the same basic laws.[106]

The Congregation of Rites had been functioning since 1587, and this had been regulating ceremonies since that time. The Council of Cambrai took note of this, and ruled that within its province the laws of Trent on relics were to be observed, as well

---

[103] ". . . Excommunicatione latae sententiae aliisque poenis et censuris" —*Loc. cit.*

[104] Clement VII, "*Ex quo in Ecclesia Dei,*" *Pontificale Romanum,* page V. Leo XIII sent out the latest revision of the Pontifical in 1888. Cf. Bliley, *Altars,* p. 40.

[105] Mansi, XXXV, 973.

[106] Mansi, XXXV, 1090.

as the other decrees passed and issued by the Roman Congregation of Rites.[107]

Other provincial Councils came later, but the laws on the cult had been crystallized by their time, so they only repeated what earlier Councils and decrees had stated.[108]

The Council of Avignon in 1725 had troubles to face, owing to the peculiar adversaries against relics in the locality at that time. The bishops of the province were told to ". . . do all required by law . . .," and they were given particular instructions to supervise the stories and the narrations that would grow up around the relics.[109] This was merely the traditional attitude of the Church, making sure that the popular anecdotes concerning such sacred things were not stretched beyond and past the bounds of solid truth. St. Augustine had done the same in the fourth century,[110] and Charles Borromaeo in the sixteenth century.[111]

A year later, the Provincial Council of Fermo (1726) reiterated the law of the Council of Trent, adding a prudent and wise instruction for the faithful to keep in mind that the main thing in the churches is the Sacrament of the Eucharist. All things else in the churches are subordinated to that—relics of the saints included. Everything in the churches is for the honor of God primarily, and the reason why there are relics is to help towards the right and due honor to God.[112] This is a clear and simple truth, heartily in accord with all the church laws of devotion.

Ten years later, in 1736, a Provincial Council for the Maronites was held at Mount Libanus. It mentioned the law of the Council of Trent as obliging upon them in their rite also, and added other particular rules for local conditions and necessities.[113] It is interesting to note that all the Western dislike for anything that resembles trafficking in relics was forbidden in this Eastern Council as well. All seeking of money through relics was

---

[107] Mansi, XXXVI *ter*, 171.

[108] C. of Mechlin, in 1607—Mansi, XXXIVb, 1458; C. of Narbonne, in 1609—Mansi, XXXIVb, 1485; C. of Bordeau, in 1624—Mansi, XXXIVb, 1549; C. of Evreux, in 1727—Mansi, XXXIVb, 1926.

[109] Mansi, XXXVI, 302.

[110] *De Civitate Dei,* XXII, 8, *MPL,* XLI, 760.

[111] C. of Milan—Mansi, XXXIVa, 184 and 207.

[112] Mansi, XXXVII, 637.

[113] Mansi, XXXVIII, 38-40.

banned, and the very words of the Tridentine Council were used to show that in the veneration there was to be nothing unfitting or indecent.[114] Their bishops had the power to approve new relics, though they were advised to refer the matter to the Patriarch for the final decision. Within two months from the day of the Council, all pastors were to send to their bishops an index or list of all the relics in their churches, together with the documents for their authenticity. These documents were to be preserved in the episcopal archives. The Patriarch was to appoint experts to examine the relics with their documents, and their final report was to be sent to the Holy See. In case that any church possessed a notable relic (*reliquia insignis*) of any martyr, either of the martyrology of Rome or Antioch, the feast-day was to be observed by the church possessing it.

Three Councils at the end of the seventeenth and the first quarter of the eighteenth century made a great step forward in the practical canonical discipline toward relics. These were the II Provincial Council of Beneventum in the year 1698,[115] the Provincial Council of Naples in 1699,[116] and the Provincial Council of Avignon in 1725.[117] These selected from the decrees of the past ". . . which were good laws, though they had not been obeyed, . . ." a set of new regulations, partly dogmatic and partly canonical. Relics are sacred things, monuments to fortitude, incentives to victory—but they must be approved by the bishops before they can be exposed for public veneration. They must be kept in a receptacle that is sealed and closed, and in a fit place. They are to be exposed only rarely, and they are not to be carried in procession or to the sick, unless the bishop give explicit permission. Only clerics in sacred Orders were allowed to touch them. Theft was forbidden under pain of excommunication; and there was to be no official publication of the miracles wrought through them, except by the bishop of the territory. This was putting into practice what Rome desired, because the

114 ". . . Nihil inordinatus, nihil profanum, nihil inhonestum, nihil praepostere, nihil tumultuarie. . . ."—*Loc. cit.*

115 *Collectio Lacensis,* I, 134.

116 *Coll. Lac.,* I, 200.

117 *Coll. Lac.,* I, 507.

decrees reflect the influence of the Congregation of Rites and the Congregation of Relics.

Even in the nineteenth century, there were other Councils which legislated upon the cult, but they added nothing new to the body of laws already in existence.[118]

In the United States of America, none of the three Provincial Councils made any mention concerning relics, probably for the simple reason that relics of the Saints were not so common in this land as in Europe, and hence were not noticeable as having any decided influence upon public devotions. The ordinary provisions of the Congregation of Rites and the Roman Ritual were sufficient legislation to cover all questions which arose, and consequently the Baltimore Councils did not give particular consideration to these matters. The regular and routine details of the episcopal visitations were in force, however, and upon those occasions, the bishops inspected the relics and the reliquaries in the parish churches, together with the documents for their authentication. Bishops were charged to see that nothing unfit would occur at their exposition, and to abolish what was unbecoming. The closet or niche where the relics were habitually kept was to be inspected, to see that it was neatly lined and fastened with a lock and key.[119]

ART. 5. ESTABLISHMENT OF ROMAN CONGREGATION FOR THE CARE OF RELICS

A. *Activities of this Congregation.* To all the laws of the Church on the cult of relics came on July 6th, 1669, when Pope Clement IX, in the Constitution *"In Ipsis,"* instituted a new and separate Congregation at Rome to oversee and supervise all matters pertaining to Indulgences and to the Relics of the Saints. As a matter of fact, this Congregation had already begun to function on August 4th, 1667, but the Holy Father did not give out the official charter and constitution for the Congregation until he was assured that it had proved its necessity and its value. Only after two years did the Pope issue the official

---

118 C. of Soissons, in 1849—Mansi, XLIII, 581; C. of Avignon, in 1849—Mansi, XLIII, 736; C. of Bourges, in 1850—Mansi, XLIV, 80.

119 *Manual of Episcopal Visitation*, p. 24.

charter of erection.[120] It contains the complete story of the foundation, as well as the reasons for the Pontiff's action in erecting this particular body.

> At the very beginning of our Pontificate, when we had found many Congregations of our venerable brother Cardinals instituted by our Predecessors in the Roman Pontificate for the good of the Church, and for the speedy and propitious transaction of the routine business that flows into the Roman Curia from all parts of the world—so as to release the Pontiff from a mountain of care—we saw no Congregation erected with the particular task of caring for the treasury of Indulgences, and for the authentication of Sacred Relics.
>
> Wishing, therefore, to manage with order all matters that touch upon this great Treasury as well as the care of Relics, we selected some Cardinals and other Prelates of the Curia, and others known for their spirituality, piety and prudence, with whose help we might be the better able to discharge this serious duty of ours for the glory of God, the honor of the Church, and the spiritual edification of the faithful in Christ.
>
> Very soon after this, as the importance of the matter demanded, the prelates came together and put forth their hand to the task committed them.
>
> We think that they have done their work very well. Hoping in the Lord that this very useful work will go on in the future, and wishing to perpetuate the fruit of the wise counsel which God has deigned to impart, and desiring that He continue to send His gift of Counsel as before, *MOTU PROPRIO*, we erect and constitute out of these aforesaid prelates a Congregation, which in the future shall be elected and deputed by us and our successors. This Congregation shall have the right to settle all difficulties and doubts in the matter of Indulgences and Relics, provided that it be not a matter pertaining to some dogma of the Faith, and provided also that in extraordinarily serious cases the Pontiff be consulted. This Congregation has the right to abolish abuses, even without the formality of a trial; but if the case be such as to demand a canonical process, it is to be remitted to the proper judges.
>
> It has the right to forbid the printing of false, apocryphal and indiscreet Indulgences, of examining and approving and

---

[120] *Decreta Authentica Sacrae Congregationis Indulgentiis Sacrisque Reliquiis Praepositae*, page V.

> rejecting, with the authority of the Pontiff, all lists that claim to be based upon Pontifical approval.
>
> It has the right, also, of examining and authenticating all new relics, which our predecessor Innocent III, in the General Council of the Lateran, forbade for public veneration unless fortified by the approval of the Pontiff.
>
> In the concession of Indulgences, and in the approval of relics of the Saints, we demand by the tenor of these letters that all be done with moderation, and with care that is prudent, pious and upright.
>
> These letters are firm, valid, . . . no other privilege of interpreting to the contrary being valid unless it be specific, express and word-for-word. . . .
>
> Given at Rome, under the Seal of the Fisherman, at St. Mary Major's, in the third year of our Pontificate, July 6, 1669.

The personnel of the Congregation consisted of six members. A Cardinal was prefect, and he had an assistant as his secretary. There were four other members who were consultors: the Sacristan of the Holy Father (who held this office *ex officio*), the secretary of the Congregation of Rites, a promotor fidei, and a prefect of ceremonies.[121]

The great scope of this Congregation may be seen from the wide faculty given it, allowing it to act with all the power of the Pontiff in ordinary cases, even without consulting the Roman Pontiff. In fact, it was not until the year 1780 that the first extraordinary case was referred to the Holy Father, and this was one hundred and eleven years after the Congregation had begun to function.[122]

It must be confessed, however, that the Congregation was asked more often to legislate upon questions affecting Indulgences than Relics. In 1883, the *"Authentic Decrees of the Sacred Congregation for Relics and Indulgences"* were printed by order of Leo XIII, and it is found that only twenty-two (22) decrees refer to relics, and the remaining four hundred thirty-five (435) to indulgences. The first decree issued by the Con-

---

[121] Laurentius, *Institutiones Iuris Ecclesiastici,* p. 123, n. 154.

[122] S. C. Indulg. et Reliq., decretum, Sept. 23, 1780—*Decr. Auth.,* n. 240—where Pope Pius VI upheld the rule made previously by the Congregation in stating that documents of authenticity written and signed by the Vicar General alone are invalid.

gregation pertained to the marks of identification whereby the graves and the relics of martyrs in the Catacombs could be discerned from others.

> When it was discussed in the *Congregation for the care of Indulgences and Relics* which were the marks distinguishing true relics of the holy martyrs from false and doubtful relics, the Congregation decided after a diligent examination that the *palm* and the *phial tinctured with their blood* are to be considered as the most certain signs of identification. The Congregation postpones until some other time the examination of other signs.[123]

This was the most important question that it could have handled, owing to the conditions of the times when it was issued, and once it was settled, there were no other particularly difficult questions that presented themselves.

Mabillon, the French Benedictine, attacked this decree of the Congregation in 1698, publishing a book which appeared first in Latin (anonymously), and later in French, under the title: *A Letter of Eusebius of Rome to Theophilus of France, on the Cult of the Unknown Saints.*[124]

In 1701, the book was hailed before the Congregation of the Index, and had not friends of Mabillon gone directly to Pope Clement XI, it probably would have been condemned. After an examination of it, the Pontiff told Mabillon to revise parts of the work and to send it out in a new edition. In 1705, this was completed, and the second edition was approved by the Pontiff and the Congregation of the Index, after the criticism of the decree had been removed.[125]

---

[123] S. C. Indulg. et Reliq., decr., April 10, 1668—*Decr. Auth.*, n. 1.

[124] *Eusebii Romani ad Theophilum Gallum, Epistola de Cultu Sanctorum Ignotorum,* Paris, 1698.

[125] Mabillon, "De Cultu Sanctorum Ignotorum," *Vetera Analecta,* p. 557. Cf. also *Dict. Théol. Cath.*, art. Mabillon, IX, 1453; Bergkamp, *Dom Jean Mabillon,* p. 95; Leclercq, art., "Ampoules de Sang," *Dict. d'Archéologie,* I, 1751. All these mention the original decree as proceeding from the Congregation of Rites, but in reality it was issued by the Congregation for Relics, n. 1, on April 10, 1668, as in the *Decreta Authentica* for that Congregation.

Cf. S. R. C., Decretum Generale, Dec. 10, 1863—*Decr. Auth.*, n. 3120—where the Congregation insisted upon adherence to the former decree of 1668, the first issued by the Congregation of Relics. It had been occa-

There were many abuses in the cult of relics at that time, in spite of the fact that only fourteen years before (1672), Pope Clement X had published a constitution, with the especial purpose of forestalling all absurdities and errors in the authentication and verification.[126] The strictest legal safeguards were thrown about the Catacombs, so as to preserve the relics from all desecration.[127] The custom of "baptizing" or "christening" relics of true Saints whose names were unknown had been allowed by the Congregation of Rites, but it was stopped as soon as abuses began. These "christened" relics had been allowed for veneration only, and the Congregation never granted the right to say a proper Mass or Office in their honor.[128] In 1691, the Congregation reaffirmed its former decrees, and by authority of Pope Innocent X forbade the recitation of a proper Office for such relics ". . . under penalty of not fulfilling the precept of Divine Office. . . ." [129]

The rule that ancient relics were to be preserved in the same veneration that they formerly enjoyed was not set up explicitly by the Congregation until the year 1864,[130] although in the year

sioned in 1863 by De Buck, who wrote *De Phialis Rubricatis* maintaining with Mabillon that all phials with red-matter did not denote a martyr's grave. Mabillon had contended that a palm *and* a phial of blood were genuine signs; Benedict XIV, *De Cultu Ss.*, t. IV, pars II, cap. 27—maintained with Boldetti that a palm *or* a phial of blood was a sufficient sign. In this point Barbier de Montault, *Oeuvres Complétes*, VII, 194, says that Benedict XIV had the correct notion, because of his authoritative interpretation of the former decree, drawn from the intention of the writers.

[126] Clement X, const. *"Ex Commissae,"* Jan. 13, 1672—*Bullarium Romanum*, XVIII, 296, ut supra, pages 48-49.

[127] Decrees of Paul V on August 24, 1613, and May 16, 1614. Cf. Lehmkuhl, *Theologia Moralis*, II, n. 710. These two laws forbade the stealing of relics, and on January 13, 1672, a censure was added as a penal sanction. Cf. *Bullarium Romanum*, XVIII, 296-298.

[128] S. R. C., *Ferrarien.*, June 7, 1681—*Decr. Auth.*, n. 1670; *Caesenaten.*, July 30, 1689—*Decr. Auth.*, n. 1815 ad 3.

[129] S. R. C., decr. gener., October 19, 1691—*Decr. Auth.*, n. 1853; Urbis et Orbis, Sept. 29, 1714—*Decr. Auth.*, n. 2228, with the same law in the same words. Cf. Zallwein, *Principia Juris Eccles.*, II, 155, on the abuses prevalent at that time.

[130] S. C. Indulg. et Reliq., *Andegaven.*, Feb. 29, 1864—*Decr. Auth.*, n. 400.

1712 the Congregation had the opportunity.[131] On this latter occasion the Congregation had been asked to grant an indulgence for those of the faithful who walked in procession with the relics of Saint Ursula. The Bishop of Placentia (in Spain) had forwarded the request for the indulgence, and along with the petition he sent this information:

> The identity of the aforesaid relics can hardly be justified by any other title than that of a most ancient cult since time immemorial. Some unsightly documents (schedulae informes) written in old characters narrate that they were brought to this city from Cologne.

The question was this: whether a plenary indulgence may be granted to those who accompany this aforesaid procession? The response was affirmative, with the restriction that nothing was stated in regard to the relics. The Congregation had not been asked to rule on their authenticity, and consequently it did not make any decision upon them. Nevertheless, the implied rule was there to the effect that ancient relics could be kept in the same devotions as formerly.

This case is illustrative of one reason why the Congregation did not issue many decrees. The difficulties in the task were often insurmountable. The natural impossibility of projecting oneself into the remote past, the physical powerlessness of determining whether particular relics really belonged to the person to whom they were ascribed, the lack of positive and written proving documents,—all these reasons and more, made the task exceedingly difficult, and at times, very precarious. Face to face with the fact of some popular devotion to a relic which had apparently nothing in its favor except a popular tradition, the Congregation had to choose its way with all the prudence and moderation enjoined upon it in its charter of erection. It had not been endowed with infallibility, or with the power to transport itself into the first centuries of the Church, and consequently, when questions were asked concerning the authenticity of relics supposed to be the remains of Saints and Martyrs long since dead, the Congregation could only act in a human way,

---

131 S. C. Indulg. et Reliq., *Placentina,* Nov. 21, 1712—*Decr. Auth.,* n. 45.

and judge from the evidences submitted whether the relic should be venerated or given a quiet burial.

There is no doubt that the Congregation was the death-knell to many fantastic and extravagant relics. It was a legal barrier and a threat against the introduction or the retention of relics which were not fitting and sacred.

In the authentication of relics there were many difficulties, and one of the greatest was the determination of a stable policy and a set rule to follow. One case in particular will show the mode of procedure established by the Congregation.[132] A parish church in the diocese of Angers had possessed from time immemorial the relics of Saint Maxentiolus, and had great popular devotion to them. There were, however, no letters of authentication to corroborate them, so the Bishop of the diocese instituted an examination of them before issuing any approval for them. During the examination of them, nothing was found to militate against the common traditions of the place. Anatomists examined the bones in the crypt, and their testimony was that all the bones, except two, belonged to the same body. These two, they said, belonged to some other body. The Bishop then sent two questions to the Congregation for solution:

> 1. Even though positive, proving letters are lacking, does not the uninterrupted possession of the body of a Saint from time immemorial, and constant public cult to the Saint, suffice for veneration to be given to Saint Maxentiolus—since these things seem to induce moral certitude?
>
> 2. What is to be done with the two bones that belong to some other body, not that of Saint Maxentiolus? Should they be extracted from the urn, or should they be left as they were before?

On February 29, 1864, the Congregation replied as follows:

> *Ad 1um.* The faithful are not to be disturbed in their devotion (fideles non sunt inquietandi).
>
> *Ad 2um.* Let there be no change from the past (nihil est innovandum).

It can be seen from this that the Congregation desired to avoid any radical changes in the popular devotions, especially when

---

[132] S. C. Indulg. et Reliq., *Andegaven.*, Feb. 20, 1864—*Decr. Auth.*, n. 400.

they had long traditions in their favor. Presumptions of fact and law both favored the authenticity of the relics, and since there was nothing unbecoming in the devotion, the Congregation allowed it to continue. It is noticed that the Congregation did not state that the relics were authentic. To have done so would have left it open to the charge that a conclusion had been drawn from evidence that was not entirely conclusive. The members of the Congregation had no way of determining anything positive about Saint Maxentiolus from the relics, and their main object in permitting the devotion to continue was not so much the authentication of the relics as the furthering of devotion to the Saint. Because the faithful had believed in this Saint's relics for years, and had performed many good works before them, the Congregation ruled that the people were not to be disturbed in their beliefs; and because the other two relics had been in the same crypt from time immemorial, along with the true relics of the Saint, the natural presumption was that they had been placed there because of some link of sacredness in common with the Saint. Nothing positive could be known about them; nothing positive could be learned against them. That being the situation, the best thing to do was to leave them alone, untouched. The rule was to let things go on as before, unless positive knowledge militated against them. That this attitude of the Congregation was successful is seen from the fact that it has been made a rule in the Code. Canon 1285 §2 is a summary of the whole method of procedure in such matters:

> Relics that are ancient are to be retained in the same veneration as they formerly had, unless in some particular case it is proved by certain arguments that they are false or supposititious.

As has been said above, the authentic decrees of the Congregation were printed and published in 1883. Some later decrees were printed in the *Collectanea Sacrae Congregationis de Propaganda Fide* (Rome, 1907), but it is impossible to say whether all the subsequent decisions were inserted therein. In 1881, the Cardinal Vicar sent instructions to prevent false relics from being authenticated, and he warned the Ordinaries of the world not to allow supposed relics from the Catacombs to be honored in public cult ". . . until they should be instructed in future letters how they ought to act in regard to these relics."

> . . . Some of them had letters of authentication, others lacked them; all of them had marks and indications which seemed to show their antiquity. After an examination of them in their cases, whatever in them seemed doubtful was taken and buried in the subterranean cemeteries. But it is to be feared that many such relics purchased at Rome, without being presented to the Cardinal Vicar of the city (who alone is competent to judge rightly and legitimately about the relics found in the underground tombs of the early Christians), were carried away to distant lands, probably with the hope that they would be approved by the bishops of those territories.
>
> Moreover, since wicked men were acquiring much money from this sacrilegious kind of traffic, they began to work out new kinds of fraud. For they fashioned caskets with supposititious relics and markings that appeared ancient which were so well arranged that they appeared like the legitimate things; nor were they afraid to forge letters testifying to their authenticity. Because of this, many people have been deceived.
>
> Not always was it granted to detect these deceits. It is to be feared that even the officials in the Lipsanotheca, deceived by the frauds, have fallen into the errors of the forgerers. Therefore, rules are now made to inquire who were the initiators of this imposture and who were their assistants.
>
> In the meantime, the duty has been assigned me (the Cardinal Vicar) by the Pontiff to warn the Bishops that bodies of martyrs, reputed to have come from the Roman cemeteries of the early Christians and now venerated in the churches, are to be considered as generally suspicious, however much they have been recognized and approved in the past. Bishops are not to allow them to be exposed to the veneration of the faithful again, until they have been told in new instructions how they are to act concerning them.[133]

The implication is that future letters were sent, but there is no trace of them in the *Collectanea,* where the present letter is found. It is very probable that particular instructions were

[133] Vicariatus Urbis, litt. encycl., Jan. 17, 1881—*Collectanea,* n. 1546.

sent to petitioning Ordinaries, and that these were private letters instead of public decrees.

The method of procedure in the Congregation was based on adherence to the laws of earlier Councils, as well as upon strict consideration for prudence and discretion. Positive signs for the truth of relics were demanded, and at times some petitions sent by Ordinaries were returned, together with the statement that although the consultors had given the question mature deliberation, more proof was required to establish the authenticity of the relics in question.[134]

B. *Amalgamation with the Congregation of Rites.* All the while that the Congregation of Relics had been functioning, there was another Roman Congregation with a scope for activities that overlapped the province of the former. This was the Congregation of Rites, erected by the constitution of Sixtus V, *"Immensae Aeterni Dei,"* January 22, 1587.[135] As early as 1619, it had made laws for the use of relics in ecclesiastical functions, as the authentic decrees show. The Congregation of Rites has given practically every rubric that touches upon the public and external veneration of relics, whether of the True Cross, or of the Passion, or of the saints and martyrs. This was a natural development, since the very honor and devotion to relics tend to become manifested in external ceremonies, and thus fall immediately into the province of the Congregation of Rites.

By the year 1904, there was no longer any need of a separate Congregation for the care of Relics, so Pius X united it with the Congregation of Rites. This was done in the constitution *"Quae in Ecclesiae bonum."*[136] Four years later, in 1908, when the same Pope reorganized the Roman Curia, the Congregation of Indulgences and Relics was abolished, and ceased to exist as a separate entity. The supervision of relics was given to the Congregation of Rites, and the care of Indulgences was entrusted to the Congregation of the Holy Office.[137]

---

[134] S. C. Indulg. et Reliq., *Atrebaten.*, Jan. 31, 1848—*Decr. Auth.*, n. 345; *Abellinen.*, April 14, 1877—*Decr. Auth.*, n. 432.

[135] *Decreta Authentica S. C. Rituum,* I, xi; Capello, *De Curia Romanà,* p. 313.

[136] *Analecta Ecclesiastica,* XII, 64; *Acta Pontificia,* I, 339.

[137] This reorganization and re-distribution of matter was effected by the constitution *"Sapienti Consilio"* of June 29, 1908—*AAS,* I (1909), 7.

Ever since the constitution *"Ex Commissae"* of Clement IX in 1672, the care and distribution of Roman relics has been in the hands of the Cardinal Vicar there. The active administration and the regular distribution of them, however, has been committed to the *Vicegerens*, or the assistant of the Cardinal Vicar. It is his duty to care for the *Lipsanotheca*, or that part of the Cardinal Vicar's palace where the large collection of relics is kept and guarded. That is the situation prevailing at the present time. "The *Lipsanotheca* is open to the public all day on the Thursday of the fifth week in Lent. . . . In the cabinets are the relics which the Cardinal Vicar distributes *gratis* to the churches or to individuals who petition for them. . . ."[138] The custom of "baptizing" or "christening" relics of Saints whose names are unknown has been revived, but the assigning of names is not completely arbitrary. An official list has been drawn up, and only those names are imposed. They are, as a rule, general names of virtues, such as St. Amator, St. Fortunatus, St. Victor and St. Verecunda.

C. *Code Laws based on decrees of these Roman Congregations.* This is the situation prevailing at the present time. The Code has given nine canons to explain and define the limits of the right devotion, and these canons have been taken almost bodily from the decrees of the aforesaid Congregations, i.e., the Congregation of Rites and the Congregation of Indulgences and Relics. The nine canons are an admirable synthesis of all the laws of the cult in its general outlines.[139]

In 1907, Pope Pius X wrote his encyclical letter against Modernism, *"Pascendi Dominici Gregis,"* and in it there are several rules for the right supervision of relics. The Vigilance Committee was warned ". . . not to overlook those pious books in which local traditions and stories of relics are narrated. Let them see that such questions are not agitated in newspapers, or in devotional books or magazines."[140]

---

[138] Barbier de Montault, *Oeuvres Complètes,* VII, 203.

[139] Canons 1281 to 1289. The law demanding relics in altars is in canon 1198.

[140] The Encyclical letter *"Pascendi,"* with its principles for the use and cult of relics, was rewritten into the other encyclical against Modernism, the *"Sacrorum Antistitum,"* on September 1, 1910, in *AAS,* II (1910), 664. Originally it was in the *Acta Sanctae Sedis,* XL, 593.

After this general instruction, the encyclical gave particular rules for the canonical discipline toward these sacred objects. The Code has accepted all of the regulations in the encyclical, and has given in canons 1284 and 1285 some rules which are pliable enough to allow the maintenance of popular and deep-rooted devotions,[141] and firm enough to allow the Bishop the right to abolish any cult and any devotion which he thinks is insufficiently supported by solid facts.[142]

---

[141] Canon 1285, §2. Reliquiae tamen antiquae in ea veneratione qua hactenus fuerunt sunt retinendae, nisi in aliquo casu peculiari certis argumentis constet eas falsas vel suppositicias esse.

[142] Canon 1284. Locorum Ordinarii reliquiam, quam certo non esse authenticam norint, a fidelium cultu prudenter amoveant.

PART II

LEGISLATION IN THE CODE OF CANON LAW

Preliminary Survey

The use and the veneration of sacred relics are mentioned in fourteen canons of the Code. Canon 1276 tells of the liceity of the veneration, and canon 1255 defines the nature of the devotion which may be paid to them. Canons 1281 and 1282 present rules on the right care of relics, and canons 1283 to 1286 treat all the questions pertaining to their authentication by ecclesiastical authorities. The exposition of relics is governed by canon 1287, but the Code does not give detailed rules for the liturgical ceremonies. Regulations concerning the relics of the True Cross which are in the pectoral crosses of Bishops are made by canon 1288. The sale and the profanation of all relics are forbidden by canon 1289, and a penal sanction against the sale or distribution of false relics is given in canon 2326. The law demanding relics in all altars is in canon 1198, and the situations in which the altars must be reconsecrated because of the violation of the relic-cavity are outlined in canon 1200.

CHAPTER III

THE CULT AND CARE OF RELICS

ART. 1. THE CATHOLIC IDEA AND IDEAL FOR THE CULT

Canon 1276. Bonum atque utile est Dei Servos, una cum Christo regnantes, suppliciter invocare eorumque reliquias atque imagines venerari . . .

Canon 1255 §2. Sacris quoque reliquiis atque imaginibus veneratio et cultus debetur relativus personae ad quam reliquiae imaginesque referuntur.

A. *The cult of Relics is not compulsory; neither is it absolutely necessary.* The Council of Trent condemned those who said that honor and veneration were not due to the relics of Saints, but it did not impose any positive command upon all persons to pay them explicit acts of homage. There is no obligation upon anyone to practise the devotion; rather is the sole obligation toward relics a negative one, that is to say, an explicit command not to dishonor them.[1] The obligation of particular individuals to show special signs of reverence and devotion does not come from any positive precept, but from ". . . quadam summa decentia."[2]

B. *The cult of Relics is honest, holy and efficacious.* Authors in Theology are accustomed to explain the liceity and the usefulness of the cult of relics from proofs in Holy Scripture, tradition and reason. In the present order of things, God uses physical agencies to transmit His acts of Providence. Of all material things, nothing is more fitting and more sacred than the relics of His Saints to be the vehicles of His works.[3] Nothing is more

[1] Sess. XXV, *de invocatione, veneratione, et reliquiis Sanctorum:* "Affirmantes Sanctorum Reliquiis venerationem atque honorem non deberi, vel eas a fidelibus inutiliter honorari, damnandos esse."

[2] Zallwein, *Principia Juris Eccles.*, II, 160.

[3] Acts, 5:15—where the shadow of St. Peter worked a miracle. Cf. also

evident in all Church history than the constant and fervent devotion to the Saints and martyrs of the Faith, beginning in Apostolic times and extending in unbroken sequence even to the present day.[4] Devotion to the Saints has always centred around their relics, and the same basic reasons are used to justify both cults.

Devotion to relics in the Catholic Church satisfies one of the natural cravings of human nature. It is the human instinct for friendship and remembrance raised to the state where natural acts become religious in character, because of the spiritual excellence of the person honored. The self-same instincts that induce and incite a person to cherish a material token of a deceased friend or a national hero will also prompt him to honor and venerate the relics of a person who lived and died in sanctity, vested with heroism in God's service. Basically, love and admiration are at the root of both actions. Possession of a memento will inspire a friend, and unite him in heart and mind with the object of his affection. The same spirit and intention are carried through civil life as well as religious life, for nations will spend much money to acquire documents or trinkets which have had some influence upon the life of the country, and museums will scour the earth in search for keepsakes of the masters of intellectual culture, however small or trivial may be the objects of their quests. The intrinsic value may be practically nothing, but through their association with a leader in the arts or the sciences they have taken on a new and added importance. Their true value is not so much what they are, but what they represent.

The same stands for the devotion to Relics in the Church. Whoever honors a relic of a Saint honors that Saint; and whoever honors a Saint does honor to God. The devotion tends not to the material particle but to the personality represented by it,

19:11—where garments were brought from St. Paul, and prodigies were accomplished through them.

[4] Bellarmine, *De Controversiis,* II, 463 ss., traces the devotion from the earliest days, indicating how this devotion was manifested at all times by public devotions, acts of pilgrimage, eulogies of bishops, translations of relics, laws demanding relics in altars, popular customs and legal enactments. Cf. also Zallwein, *Principia Juris Eccles.,* II, 162; Lugo, *de Mysterio Incarnationis,* Disp. XXXVII.

and in that respect is the devotion to relics a relative one. Veneration of a statue or an image passes through and beyond the cold marble, and reaches the person whose representation it is; devotion to relics passes through and beyond the material particles and becomes an act of cult to the person whose relics they are. An act of devotion made directly to a Saint is an act of perfect *dulia;* an act of devotion made before the relic of the Saint would be an act of imperfect *dulia.* The one is directed immediately toward the person; the other is directed immediately toward his relic. In like manner are there acts of perfect and imperfect *latria* toward Christ or toward a relic of Christ; similarly there can be perfect or imperfect *hyperdulia* toward the Virgin Mary or toward her relics.[5] The Code in canon 1255 §2 prefers the word *relative* to *imperfect.* Both have the same meaning in this context.

The Church has always avoided that crude animism which imagines a mystic reservoir of hidden power in relics; rather has the middle course been chosen, avoiding the excesses on the one side and the defects on the other, together with all the obstacles placed by friends and foes. There have been many abuses, mostly traceable to the overflow of sentimentality and emotion in particular individuals who pushed the natural inclinations too far. Abuses are always wrong, it is true, but when they are committed in good faith, as most of them were, there is some palliation for them.

The main purpose of the cult of relics is to honor the saints, and not merely to ask miracles from God. Many times, indeed, has God rewarded the devotion by working miracles through the relics, but that is quite apart from the essential features of the cult,—though God has often joined one with the other as a recompense for the good faith or as a manifestation of His glory. In theory, however, a person who honors a relic has not an egoistic end in view, but rather an altruistic; he venerates, not to receive, but to give; and the object of his devotion is not his own personal aggrandizement, but the increasing of honor to a Saint of God. Concomitant with that, it is true, there may often be a wish or a prayer for a favor from God, and the history of

[5] Lugo, *De Mysterio Incarnationis,* disp. XXXVII, sect. III, n. 25.

the Church is filled with incidents which show how God has rewarded devotion to relics by miraculous intervention of His power. The miracle is not done by the relic; it is done by God, working through the relic and recompensing the devotion done to the Saint.

The cult of relics has been accused of being indecent and morbid, unworthy of place in the true Faith. To many, the idea of dissecting the remains of a Saint, and distributing the minute bone-particles far and wide seems the very essence of morbid depravity and misled religious mania. If the reason for all this were commercial or mercenary, even the Catholic would give his firm assent; when all this is done reverently and quietly, however, there is nothing unfit in it. This is the underlying principle of all Church laws permitting the cult, and it is a practise sanctioned by traditions that began with the martyrs of the Coliseum and of the gladiatorial games. Relics are sacred particles, and they are to be handled sacredly. Placing a small portion of a martyr's bone inside a glass-covered reliquiary is far from being repugnant to sound religious thinking, especially when the motivating and directing principle is the intention of furthering the honor of that Saint. As men are constituted, they are more easily moved and inspired when they have before their eyes some tangible and visible incentive, than when they have nothing except a purely mental inducement or intellectual urge.

Always did the Church insist that nothing indecent was to be honored, and that fitness was a prime requisite in every article offered for public veneration. Relic-cult was not a devotion established by law; it was rather a natural practise permitted by Her. The Church was outside the cult, so to speak, in a position to regulate it when it tended to extremes or to encourage it when the occasion arose. This "stand-off" attitude shows in the laws which the Church was called upon to make. In the majority of cases, they were not laws regulating future policy, except insofar as they were regulations directed for or against practises already existing; and consequently many indecencies had the opportunity to gain a momentum which was very difficult to overcome, once the popular fancy had been attracted. For abuses such as these, the Church can receive no condemnation; the fault is with human nature, not with the Church.

Even in the latter case, however, it is not right to be too severe in the judgments of acts and decisions made long ago and far away, particularly when the norm for measuring decency is changeable and inconstant. The word "indecency" can hardly be defined with rigorous exactness, capable of a universal application. It is a variable term, and may be determined in its precise meaning by the circumstances of time and place and conditions. What was decent in the fourth or the tenth century may not be decent in the twentieth; what is decent in the twentieth century in one land may be indecent in another. The variable conditions of time and mental attitudes modify the requirements for fitness and right proportion. It is true that there is a fundamental note of constancy and firmness and stability running through all men at all times, but it is also true that human nature is so led by the emotions that men will often obey their feelings rather than their reason, and at the same time be convinced that they have chosen the right course. Here is the attitude of sincerity and good faith, at work on a line of action (or scheme of devotion) which may be objectively wrong. There is need of a guide in such matters, in order to keep the right balance and the steady path. That guide in the cult of relics is the Ordinary of the diocese. To him there has been committed the spiritual care and direction of the faithful, and in the matter of relics he must follow the path set down by the canons of the Code. Canons 1281 to 1289 are the synthesized wisdom of twenty centuries of dearly-bought experience, and are an admirable summary of all laws on this devotion.

The Church has allowed the privileges of a special Mass and Office for feasts of the Commemoration of Sacred Relics of the Saints. The date is variable. With the Benedictines it is on the thirtieth day of November;[6] in Poland, on the Sunday after the feast of St. Matthew;[7] in Basle, on the Sunday in the octave of All Saints' day.[8] In 1912, however, the Congregation of Rites sent out some solutions to doubts concerning the new rubrics issued at the time, and transferred the feast of the Commemora-

---

[6] S. R. C., *Einsiedeln.*, May 5, 1736—*Decr. Auth.*, n. 2319 ad 15*um*.

[7] S. R. C., *Varsavien.*, May 7, 1746—*Decr. Auth.*, n. 2390.

[8] S. R. C., *Basilien.*, March 6, 1896—*Decr. Auth.*, n. 3892.

tion of Sacred Relics—wherever it had been heretofore celebrated on a Sunday—to a new fixed date on the fifth of November.[9] This last date is the most commonly observed.

ART. 2. THE CARE OF RELICS

Canon 1281 §1. Insignes reliquiae aut imagines pretiosae itemque aliae reliquiae aut imagines quae in aliqua ecclesia magna populi veneratione honorentur, nequeunt valide alienari neque in aliam ecclesiam perpetuo transferri sine Apostolicae Sedis permissu.

§2. Insignes Sanctorum vel Beatorum reliquiae sunt corpus, caput, brachium, antibrachium, cor, lingua, manus, crus aut illa pars corporis in qua passus est martyr, dummodo sit integra et non parva.

Canon 1282 §1. Insignes Sanctorum vel Beatorum reliquiae neque in aedibus vel oratoriis privatis asservari, sine expressa Ordinarii loci licentia.

§2. Reliquiae non insignes debito cum honore etiam in domibus privatis servari pieque a fidelibus gestari possunt.

A. *No alienation of notable relics without proper permission.* The Congregation of Relics was asked on November 17, 1676, whether a bishop could give permission to have relics transferred from one place to another that was more fitting, on account of increase of devotion to them. The reply was that the bishop may permit any such transfers within the same church, but that he could not allow relics to be alienated or transferred outside the diocese without the permission of the Roman Pontiff.[10] This was a law partly new and partly old. It had been in the *Decretum Gratiani*, [11] and before that, in the laws of the Council of Mayence, in 813.[12]

---

[9] S. R. C., *Dubia*, Feb. 9, 1912—*AAS*, IV (1912), 106.

[10] S. C. Indulg. et Reliq., decr., Nov. 17, 1676—*Decr. Auth.*, n. 14.

[11] C. 37, D. I, *de consecratione.*

[12] Canon 51—Let no one presume to transfer the bodies of the Saints from one place to another, without the consent of the secular prince or the bishops, and the permission of the Synod.—Labbe, *Concilia*, VII, 1253.

The Code forbids the permanent disposal of these notable relics to any other church, whether within the diocese or outside it. Not even the local Bishop is competent to grant permission allowing a permanent transfer, even within his own diocese, for the reason that the Code presumes all such notable relics to be closely allied and associated with the church which possesses them.

Temporary transfer or disposal, however, is not forbidden so strictly as the permanent alienation, but even for this there must be a just and proportionate cause, as the law implies. The judge of the sufficiency of these causes is not necessarily the Apostolic See, since the Code does not state or insinuate that; accordingly, the local Ordinary may give his decision on the merit of the reasons for the temporary change or transfer. The law of Gratian may be followed in this matter:

> For three causes, the [resting] places of the Saints may be changed: first, when persecutors threaten them; second, when their location becomes disadvantageous; third, when they are in a place that has become less fit on account of evil men.[13]

For these reasons, temporary transfer of notable relics could be allowed, either within the diocese or outside it. In the latter case, both Ordinaries would be competent to judge and decide on the sufficiency of the causes for the temporary change of location.

The law affects primarily the prominent or notable relics (which are enumerated in the second paragraph of this canon), but it also affects other relics not so intrinsically important, but towards which there is great popular devotion in some particular church.

---

[13] C. 36, D. I, *de consecratione*. Cf. Craisson, *Manuale*, I, n. 1030, demanding permission of the Pontiff or the Congregation of Rites even in such cases. The law of the Code in canon 1281 does not require this, nor does any positive law of the Congregation of Rites and the Congregation of Relics. Reiffenstuel, lib. III, tit. 43, n. 32—held that the Ordinary could allow permanent disposal to another church in the same diocese. This latter opinion is untenable at present, because canon 1281 is directly opposing it; the former opinion (Craisson) is more strict than the Code, and hence need not be urged as obligatory.

The Code speaks only of popular devotion to such relics in *churches*, but it is in accord with the intent of the law to extend this term so as to include all other sacred places of worship, such as the chapels in a convent, or seminary, or college.

Some such place as this might possess only a small relic of its patron or some other Saint, but nevertheless if there is great popular devotion to it, even that small relic could not be taken away or given away without the permission of the Holy See. The disposal of such a relic without proper permission would be invalid, without legal effect in any forum. All such indults or permissions to alienate relics will come from the Congregation of the Council, which has complete competence in all matters that affect the disposition of *bona ecclesiastica, mobilia et immobilia.*[14]

What if the church itself does not own the relic in question? It might happen that a pastor or assistant-priest would acquire a relic in his own name, and commence public devotions to it in his church. There might arise great reverence and veneration to it. With that situation existing, could the pastor or the priest dispose of that relic as he pleased, on the grounds that it was his own property, and not that of the church? The Code says he may not do so. He was not obliged to commence public services in its honor, but once he has, the relic itself became public property, with its title resting in the church.The people have acquired or prescribed the right to venerate it.

This might find practical application where there are many devotions to the relics of St. Ann, St. Rita, St. Theresa and others. If a priest who possessed one of these relics should be transferred to another parish, could he take the relics with him? The Code says he may not do so, if there exists great popular devotion to it in the first parish. But would this same priest always be obliged to give up his title to the relic? Situations might vary in different cases, but it seems right and equitable to say that if the former parish has another similar relic of the same Saint, the priest in the example is not obliged to relinquish his own. The faithful have shown devotion to the relics of the

[14] Cocchi, *Commentarium,* III, n. 113; Blat, *Commentarium,* II, 184.

Saint, but not to any particular or specific relic, unless it be an exceptional case. If the devotion would be just as real and true toward another relic of the same Saint, then the first relic is not so intimately connected with the cult that it is essential for its continuance.

The canon does not state explicitly who is judge of the situations as they stand, but the whole trend of the title in which this canon appears indicates that the Ordinary is competent to supervise all matters that pertain to public cult in the diocese. His powers cease where the law demands permission from the Holy See, but where the law does not make that provision, his power as Ordinary is sufficient to establish his right of jurisdiction.

B. *Notable and non-notable relics.* The term *reliquia insignis* is used by the Code to denote the most important class of relics. There is no English word with the exact shade of meaning as *insignis,* but the word *notable* approaches most closely to the Latin term. A common and prevailing view seems to be that it means *first-class,* but this last translation is not correct, and is destroyed by the very wording of the Code in this paragraph. All notable relics are first-class, since all are parts of the body of a saint; not all first-class relics, however, are notable. First-class relics of saints may be small and minute, while notable relics must have a certain volume or quantity.

The second paragraph of canon 1281 enumerates all notable relics. They are: the complete body of the saint, or the head, arm, forearm, heart, tongue, hand or leg, or that part of the body in which the saint suffered death, provided that it be entire and not a small portion. The list is taxative, i.e., no other Saint's relic besides those mentioned can be considered as notable.

This law of the Code appeared first in a decree of the Congregation of Rites, forty years before the Congregation for the care of Relics had come into existence.[15] It had been occasioned by abuses then existing in Rome itself. In October of that same year, the same Congregation had to explain some doubts and disputes not settled by its former decree in April. Asked whether the ashes of the saints were notable relics, and how much of the ashes was required before there was a notable

[15] S. R. C., *Urbis.,* April 8, 1628—*Decr. Auth.,* n. 460.

relic, the Congregation replied that it was unwilling to give a general answer to this general question, but that it would give particular responses to whatever cases were submitted.[16] Many times later was this first decree of 1628 mentioned.

In 1631, it was reprinted and reaffirmed by Pope Urban VIII, who ordered that it be printed in the new breviaries so that its precepts would be better known and better observed.[17]

Even after 1628 there were many doubts about the importance of relics in different churches, and the Congregation gave definite solutions on several occasions. Their responses to the doubts proposed make up the present law in the Code.

In 1662 it was ruled that the *tibia*, or shin-bone, was not a notable relic, and the Congregation decided this "according to the rules printed in the Missal and Breviary."[18] Neither was the thigh-bone alone considered as a notable relic.[19] In the cathedral of Padua there were relics which had been considered as notable for more than two hundred years, though they were only small portions of the thigh-bone. The Congregation of Rites, however, ruled that these were not notable relics, nor could they be made notable by any custom, however long it had continued.[20]

Other relics nevertheless, were recognized as notable, such as the fore-arm alone, and the upper portion of the arm (from the shoulder to the elbow). If by a miracle, the hand, heart or tongue of some saint had been preserved intact, they could all be considered as notable.[21]

The relic, to be notable, must be entire (*integra*). Part of the head or of the hand would not be a notable relic, though it would still be a first-class relic. Moreover, the relic must not be mutilated, or lacking its entirety. This provision of the law dates back to 1672, when the right for a special Office to a mutilated relic was denied, because the component parts of it had been

---

[16] S. R. C., *Urbis.*, October 16, 1628,—*Decr. Auth.*, n. 477 ad 10*um*.
[17] S. R. C., *Urbis et Orbis*, January 13, 1631,—*Decr. Auth.*, n. 555 ad 3*um*.
[18] S. R. C., *ad dubium*, June 3, 1662,—*Decr. Auth.*, n. 1234 ad 2*um*.
[19] S. C. Indulg. et Reliq., June 11, 1822—*Decr. Auth.*, n. 251.
[20] S. R. C., *Patavina*, December 7, 1844—*Decr. Auth.*, n. 2883 ad 1*um*.
[21] S. R. C., *Urbis et Orbis*, June 27, 1899,—*Decr. Auth.*, n. 4041.

lost.[22] The policy of the Congregation can be seen from its reply in this last case. ". . . The decree of 1628 . . . is to be observed to the strict letter." It did not say, however, that mutilated relics could not be notable, for it allowed that rating, if the relics could be joined together so as to form a complete unit. Thus if the martyr had been crushed to death and his skull smashed, the head would be a notable relic if all the competent parts were collected and assembled.

It must be remembered that this canon does not deny that parts of a saint's body are real relics, but only that not all of its parts are to be held as notable. The distinction between notable and non-notable relics is important in this respect, that churches which possess a notable relic are the recipients of special privileges denied to others.

C. *Notable relics not to be kept by private persons.* Notable relics of the saints or of the beatified may not be preserved in private homes or private oratories, without the express permission of the local Ordinary.

Since a notable relic is always an important part of a saint's body, it is right and fit that no irreverence come to it in any way. "Sancta sancte tradenda" has always been a rule of the Church of God. The only place really fit for a notable relic of a saint is a church. In ages past, many abuses began when people took these sacred remains into their homes, and many laws of old councils commanded that relics be brought to the churches and deposited there.[23] In the Code, there is the general law against the retention of notable relics in private possession. Even private oratories may not have a notable relic, unless there is express permission of the local Ordinary. There would be less unfitness, however, in keeping a notable relic in an oratory than in a private house, and consequently there would be more leniency in the granting of such permission.

If one Ordinary has granted permission of this kind, his suc-

---

[22] S. R. C., *ad Ruben.*, December 3, 1672,—*Decr. Auth.*, n. 1460.

[23] Mansi, XXV, 34—C. of Constance, in 1300; IV Conc. Milan, in 1576, in Mansi, XXXIVa, 207; C. of Bourges, in 1584, Mansi, XXXIVa, 888. Benedict XIV, *De Beatific. et Canoniz. So.*, lib. IV, pars 2, cap. 26, n. 2, repeated this same law, but made exceptions for noted civil rulers and prelates of the church.

cessor may revoke it and recall it. The whole trend of the law, both in the past as well as in the new Code, centralizes the supervision of local customs in the Ordinary, and makes him responsible for the preservation of fitness in the cult. If the successor of the Ordinary should think that the cause of the Church would be bettered by taking a relic from its present possessor and restoring it to the public property of the Church, he would be justified in doing so, and there would not be any possible question about the validity or the liceity of his act. In this matter, no Ordinary can bind his successor, because the actual superior always has to supervise present conditions which may not have been foreseen by the predecessors.

A private individual who in times past acquired a notable relic must submit to the new law in the Code, and seek express permission to retain it. Favors granted before the Code in the matter of relics do not exist as *jura quaesita,* and hence the possessor must petition the Ordinary for due permission.[24]

When the Ordinary has given permission to keep a notable relic in a private house or oratory, it need not be written, although sound policy would advise that it be done in that way. Permissions given only verbally are often difficult to prove externally, and a written document, on the contrary, presents visible and tangible evidence of a fact accomplished and allowed.

Must the possessor of such a relic obtain new permission to keep it every time there is a new Ordinary? It seems that new permission is not required, unless the conditions have so changed that the relic is in a different status than it was beforehand, at the time that the first authorization was granted. In case of doubt, new permission ought to be obtained, and the Ordinary is within his rights in demanding this. The Ordinary is the only local authority competent to give a definite statement concerning the right to keep notable relics in private custody.[25]

D. *Other relics allowed to private persons.* Relics that are not notable, according to the classifications set in in the first

[24] Vermeersch-Creusen, *Epitome,* II, n. 611.

[25] Conc. Trident., sess. XXV, *de invocatione, veneratione et reliquiis sanctorum, et sacris imaginibus*—giving the bishops the right to supervise the cult of relics, and to enforce the laws concerning them.

paragraph of this canon, may be kept in private houses by the faithful, provided that due honor be paid to them. They may be carried on one's person also, if this be done with reverence, and without superstition or affectation.

The reason for this concession is the desire of the Church to allow the faithful every possible means of personal santification, by permitting them to have in their possession constantly some visible and tangible remembrances of the saints. The inspirational value of relics, and the pious resolves which they incite are sufficient reasons to justify this concession. Notable relics belong to the Church at large, and should be kept in a public place, such as a church, so that all the faithful may have the opportunity of venerating them; but smaller relics may fittingly be owned by private persons, to be a constant reminder of the saint.

But there must not be any irreverence or superstition in this private possession. The Code says that the devotion must be pious and honorable, i.e., *pie . . . debito cum honore,* but does not go farther in indicating which honors would be fitting and proper. The habit of wearing relics in a locket suspended around the neck has always been a favorite practise in the past. St. Gregory of Tours mentioned this,[26] and it is known that Charlemagne wore such a reliquary enclosing a part of the True Cross. St. Thomas Aquinas allowed such a practise to be licit,[27] and the Congregation of Rites has at times granted permission for it.[28] As long as the sense of fitness and the sentiments of innate reverence are followed, there can hardly be any excess capable of doing much public or private harm. The Code presumes that the Ordinary will oversee all such matters, and not merely in a passive way, but positively and actively. The Church has learned how abuses can spring up, and just as in the past there were laws against the private retention of relics,[29] so now will the Church be ready to pass similar laws,

[26] *De Gloria Martyrum,* I, 5—*MPL,* LXXI, 709. Cf. also St. John Chrysostom in his homily, *Quod Christus sit Deus,* 10, *MPG,* XLVIII, 826, mentioning such reliquaries of the True Cross.

[27] *Summa Theologica,* II, IIae, q. 96, art. 4, ad 3um.

[28] S. R. C., *Naples,* May 24, 1594; Grandclaude, *Jus Canonicum,* II, 673.

[29] Synod of Constance (1300), Mansi, XXV, 34.

in case that permissions already granted would cause the same excesses as in other times.

The relics of those persons who have died in sanctity may be honored privately by the individual faithful, even though they have not been approved or authenticated.[30] "Thus it is allowed . . . to carry them on one's person, to wear them around the neck, to kiss them, or to venerate them with any similar private devotion."[31]

The local Ordinary has the right and the duty of supervising these private devotions, whenever they become numerous or widespread.

---

[30] Reiffenstuel, lib. III, tit. 45, n. 29; Craisson, *Manuale*, I, n. 1025.
[31] Reiffenstuel, *loc. cit.*

CHAPTER IV

THE AUTHENTICATION AND APPROVAL OF RELICS

Canon 1283 §1. Publico cultu eae solae reliquiae in ecclesiis, quamquam exemptis, honorari possunt, quas genuinas esse constet authentico documento alicuius S.R.E. Cardinalis, vel Ordinarii loci, vel alius viri ecclesiastici cui facultas authenticandi indulto apostolico sit concessa.

§2. Vicarius Generalis nequit, sine mandato speciali, reliquias authenticas edicere.

Canon 1284. Locorum Ordinarii reliquiam, quam certo non esse authenticam norint, a fidelium cultu prudenter amoveant.

Canon 1285 §1. Sacrae reliquiae, quarum authenticitatis documenta ob civiles perturbationes vel ob alium quemlibet casum interierint, publicae venerationi ne exponantur, nisi praecedat iudicium Ordinarii loci, non autem Vicarii Generalis sine mandato speciali.

§2. Reliquiae antiquae tamen in ea veneratione qua hactenus fuerunt, sunt retinendae, nisi in aliquo peculiari casu certis argumentis constet eas falsas vel suppositicias esse.

Canon 1286. Locorum Ordinarii ne sinant, maxime in sacris concionibus, libris, ephemeridibus vel commentariis fovendae pietati destinatis, ex meris conjecturis, ex solis probabilibus argumentis vel praejudicatis opinionibus, praesertim verbis ludibrium aut despectum sapientibus, quaestiones agitari de sacrarum reliquiarum authenticitate.

A. *Relics for public veneration need authentication and approval.* Catholic churches are public places of devotion, and they ought not shelter anything which would detract from the cause of religion. Even the relics of the Saints must be subject to some scrutiny before they may be admitted to places in the devotional practises of the Church. Lest there be credulous judgments in attributing to martyrs all the human remains found, the Holy See instituted laws as early as 1672, placing all the authentication of relics found in the Catacombs in the hands of the Cardinal Vicar of Rome.[1] This was not the first law of that nature, because Pope Alexander III, in 1170, reserved to the Pontiff the sole right of allowing veneration to newly-found relics, and Gregory IX took the same law into his Decretals.[2]

These laws, however, affected only relics newly-found, or those presented to the Church for their first authentication. Other relics which had been in constant veneration could be authenticated and approved by the local Ordinaries, and the laws of the Decretals did not take away this power which had been used by the bishops since the earliest days of the Church.[3]

The same law stands in the Code, with the added provision that all authentication take the form of a written document. This is a legal barrier to safeguard reverence and to exclude impostures.

Canon 1283 does not distinguish between the authentication of relics and their approval for public veneration, but for the sake of clarity in this commentary the distinction is made. Every relic exhibited for veneration in a public place of worship must

---

[1] Clement X, const. *"Ex Commissae,"* Jan. 13, 1672—*Bullarium Romanum,* XVIII, 296.

[2] C. 1, 2, X, *de reliquiis et veneratione Sanctorum,* III, 45.

[3] Reiffenstuel, *Jus Canonicum,* lib. III, tit. XLV, n. 7—"Before the present solemn rite of canonization was introduced, many saints were declared canonized after their death by the common consent of the Bishops and people. . . . It was a canonization process introduced by custom, by the judgment and consent of the Pope and the universal, inerrant Church. . . . The first Pope who is mentioned as solemnly canonizing saints is Leo III, elected in 796. . . . Formerly each Bishop could canonize a Saint for his own diocese, and he could order that public cult be shown him. Today all this power is taken away from the bishops, and it is reserved to the Pontiff alone." This shows that the right to canonize saints was accompanied by the legal right to authenticate and approve their relics for veneration.

be authenticated by a competent ecclesiastical official and approved by the local Ordinary.

1. *Documents for authenticity of a relic.* Canon 1283 §1 enumerates the persons competent to issue documents of authenticity. Cardinals are first on the list, by reason of their close association with the Papal household, and the unity of their power and intention with that of the Pontiff.

All local Ordinaries except the Vicar General may also authenticate. Accordingly, the following persons may issue these documents: residential Bishops, any *Abbas* or *Praelatus nullius,* Administrators, Vicars or Prefects Apostolic.[4] Vermeersch said (before the Code) that Prefects Apostolic may not authenticate, since this is an exceptional power, not necessary for the active administration of their territory.[5] According to the present law, however, the right of authenticating has been extended to the Prefects Apostolic. It may not be a necessary power, but it is a useful power, and for that reason the Code has allowed it to them.

Others who may authenticate are those ecclesiastical persons who have an apostolic indult to do so. The Congregation of Rites is the usual source of these indults, since it has competence in matters of relics.[6] The Cardinal Vicar of Rome acts habitually through his *Vicegerens* in authenticating relics from the Catacombs. In like manner also are the Major Superiors of religious Orders or Institutes sometimes given the right to authenticate relics, but ordinarily their powers are restricted to relics of the Saints or the Blessed from their own religious Institute.[7]

All prelates or officials who authenticate must take every pos-

[4] Canon 198. By the fact that canon 1283 §1 excludes Vicars General from the right to authenticate unless a special mandate is given them by the Ordinary, it seems right also to restrict this privilege of authenticating to the residential Bishops, *Abbas* and *Praelatus nullius,* Administrators, Vicars and Prefects Apostolic, without extending the right to those others mentioned as Ordinaries in canon 198, i.e., ". . . those others who, according to the prescripts of the law or from approved constitutions, succeed the above mentioned in their absence. . . ." The Code desires to make the authentication of relics a personal duty of the Ordinary, as far as possible.

[5] *Periodica,* VII, (43).

[6] Pius X, const. *"Sapienti Consilio,"* June 29, 1908—*AAS,* I (1909), 7.

[7] Vermeersch-Creusen, *Epitome,* II, n. 612.

sible means to ascertain the genuineness of the relics submitted to them. When the Saint lived within recent times, this task may be easy, and it may be possible to have strong physical certitude in the identification of the relics. When there are difficulties present, the Ordinary should summon to his assistance ". . . theologians and other pious men . . ." so as to reach a verdict in conformity with truth and piety.[8] It will be the duty of these advisers to indicate with certainty the exact body or relics of the Saints. Unless they can do so, the Ordinary has no right to authenticate. Any probability, however strong it may be, is not sufficient to permit an Ordinary to authenticate relics for the first time. Only strong moral certitude, and that alone, will suffice.[9] Unless the cult commence in the right way, it has little chance of continuing that way.

There is no set formula for the documents of authenticity. The majority of those now in use are patterned upon that employed by the Cardinal Vicar of Rome. The following is a model now in use. The formal words in the title of the document are here omitted:

> Universis et singulis praesentes litteras inspecturis fidem facimus ac testamur, quod Nos ad majorem Omnipotentis Dei gloriam suorumque Sanctorum venerationem recognovimus sacras particulas *ex ossibus S.* . . . . . quas ex authenticis locis extractas reverenter collocavimus in *theca metallica rotundae formae,* crystallo munita, bene clausa et funiculo serico coloris rubri colligata, ac sigillo nostro signata, easque tradidimus, cum facultate apud se retinendi, extra Urbem transmittendi et publicae Fidelium venerationi exponendi. Monemus autem fideles in quorum manus hae sacrae reliquiae nunc vel in posterum venturae sunt, nullo modo eas licere vendere, nec cum iis rebus quae mercimonii speciem praeseferant, commutare.
>
> In quorum fidem has litteras testimoniales manu nostra subscriptas nostroque sigillo firmatas per infrascriptum Sacrarum Reliquiarum Custodem expediri mandavimus.
>
> Romae ex Aedibus nostris Die . . . Mensis . . . Anni MCM .
>
> (*Locus Sigilli*)
>
> Reg. N . . . Gratis Quocumque Titulo

[8] Conc. Trident., sess. XXV, *de invocatione et reliquiis sanctorum, et reliquiis sanctorum, et sacris imaginibus.* Cf. also Reiffenstuel, lib. III, tit. XLV, n. 27.

[9] Bargilliat, *Praelectiones Juris Canonici,* (edit. 1913), I, n. 575 a.

The translation of this formula is as follows:

> To each and all who are to see these letters, we inform and attest that for the greater glory of God and the veneration of His Saints, we have identified sacred particles from the bones of Saint . . . , which, extracted from authentic places, we have reverently deposited in a round metal capse, covered with glass, well-enclosed, fastened upon a red silken cord and signed with our seal. We give these with permission to keep on one's self, to carry outside the city, and expose to the public cult of the faithful. We warn the faithful into whose hands these sacred relics may fall, either now or in the future, that it is not allowed to sell them in any way, or to exchange them for other things in transactions which have the appearance of commerce. We have commanded that these testimonial letters, signed with our hand and sealed with our seal, be issued through the undersigned Custodian of Sacred Relics.
>
> Given at Rome, at our Palace, on the ... day of ..., 19 ...
>
> (Place of the Seal)
>
> Signed, ...

All local Ordinaries except Vicars General may issue these documents. The reason for this exclusion seems to be the desire to centralize the control of relics in each territory in one person, who will be directly responsible for the right observance. The Code admits the right to delegate this power to the Vicars General, but it must be done by a special and express mandate. Verbal permission will suffice, but tacit or presumed permission will not. Whether the Ordinary may delegate this power to any other person than the Vicar General is not stated in the Code. Reasons may be brought to favor both affirmative and negative responses, but it seems more in accord with the historical trend of the legislation to state that this power should not be delegated. It is the wish and the desire of the Church to protect the cult from abuses, and this can be better accomplished if the right of authenticating be considered as purely personal. The Ordinary may consult other persons on the advisability and the possibility of issuing such documents, but his own name should be affixed to them. "The signature must be by hand, and not with a [rubber] stamp, unless the prelate is notoriously prevented from writing by paralysis or other bodily infirmity." [10]

These documents of verification and authentication are based on the plausibility of the evidence presented. A signed and sealed letter of authenticity never assumes the nature of an infallible decision that the relic is true. The objective truth of the document rests upon the objective truth of the relic; and if historical research or investigation should ever show that the relic is false, the Church is always willing and anxious to remove the erroneous thing from public cult. There is no question of wilful deceit being tolerated, since Canon 1284 rules that the Ordinaries are to remove from public cult all relics which are found to be spurious. It may sometimes happen that statements or documents which have been based on apparently solid and reasonable assurance will be found to lack a true foundation, because of the deceitful nature of the evidences and the witnesses. Just as controversies over the status of persons never become a *res judicata*,[11] so also does a decision of authenticity for a relic never constitute it as beyond all doubt or suspicion. It is never absolutely final, and may always be overthrown by the introduction of certain evidence to the contrary. All evidences adduced to the contrary, however, are of no avail unless they are clearly convincing, because all legal presumptions are in favor of the documented relic.

Thurston says: "The Church has never pronounced that any particular relic, not even that commonly venerated as the wood of the Cross, is authentic; but she approves of honor being paid to those relics which with reasonable probability are believed to be genuine, and which are invested with due ecclesiastical sanctions." [12]

This appears to be misleading and mistaken, especially in view of the documents themselves, all of which have such words as these: *recognovimus sacras particulas, ex authenticis locis extractas, extractas ex authenticis locis et legitime recognitas.* It

[10] Augustine, *A Commentary,* VI, 250; Barbier de Montault, *Oeuvres Complétes,* VII, 177.

[11] Canon 1902. Numquam transeunt in rem iudicatam causae de statu personarum. . . .

[12] Cf. "Relics," *Cath Encyl.,* XII, 735.

is quite true that the Church has in mind primarily the permitting of public devotion to relics thus documented, but to say that there is absolutely no pronouncement of authenticity in any such verification does not seem correct, especially when the wording of the declaration testifies to that very thing. Belief in the truth of any authenticated relic is not commanded under penalty of any dogmatic censure, but neither is disbelief with any sufficient reason entirely inculpable. The relic merits credence in proportion to the value of the human historical arguments supporting it; the stronger are its foundations the greater is its claim to respect. There is no command to venerate any particular relic, but there is a command not to dishonor and to respect those which have documents of authenticity in their favor. It is not true to say that the Church has never authenticated a relic.

In the examination of relics supposed to have come from the Roman Catacombs, the Ordinary should not proceed to any authentication. Apart from the obvious fact that a foreign Ordinary has no possibility of proving that the relic really came from the Catacombs, the Holy See has issued a positive warning on this point. After the year 1870, so many relics were stolen, counterfeited, duplicated and transported to all parts of the world that all Ordinaries were warned to take care lest they be deceived in issuing documents for supposedly Roman relics of the Catacombs. Local Ordinaries ought to send all such relics to Rome for an authentication by the Cardinal Vicar, or else ask the same prelate for instructions in the right procedure toward these relics.[13]

Local Ordinaries may authenticate the relics of any canonized or beatified person, even though the relics were never before authenticated. This is a relaxation of the former law in the Decretals which demanded that the first authentication of such relics be done by the Holy See.[14] They are not allowed to authenticate relics of persons who are not yet canonized or

[13] Vicariatus Urbis, litt. encycl., Jan. 17, 1881—*Collectanea*, n. 1546.

[14] Reiffenstuel, lib. III, tit. XLV, n. 27. The old law was changed at the Council of Trent, sess. XXV, *de invocatione, veneratione et reliquiis sanctorum, et sacris imaginibus,* and remains as such in the Code.

beatified, since this would be a recognition granting their right to public cult. They ought, however, to separate and guard the relics of persons whose causes of beatification are to be introduced, or actually are at present before the Holy See. This is not an act of public approbation, but rather a prudential move to forestall future doubts and difficulties.[15]

2. *Approbation of relics by local Ordinaries.* In addition to the documents for authenticity, every relic exhibited for public veneration must have the approval and the permission of the local Ordinary in every territory where it is offered for veneration. Even though they have been attested as genuine by other prelates, whether in Rome or elsewhere, they must be submitted to the local Ordinary for his approbation. Any Ordinary may reject relics which do not appear genuine. This last principle came in an important decision. Two questions were proposed to the Congregation of Indulgences and Relics:

> 1°. Has every Bishop outside of Rome the right to authenticate all relics whatsoever in his own diocese?
>
> 2°. May sacred relics of saints authenticated by any bishop in Italy (if no note of error or falsity is seen in their subscription, their seal and their reliquary) be rejected by any other foreign bishop, and even confiscated or prevented from being exposed to public veneration?

To both of the questions, the Congregation returned an affirmative answer.[16] "Even though the relics have been approved by the Pope, they must be examined and approved by the local Ordinary,—not that he may approve them again, but rather that he may discover whether they have really been approved at Rome, or whether there is any fraud connected with them." [17]

Documents issued by religious superiors who act with powers granted them in a special indult always have the inserted clause: "retinendi . . . donandi . . . et in quolibet templo exponendi *de consensu Ordinarii* . . ." in order to show that the local Ordinary must grant his approval before the relic is to be exhibited in public services. The fact that this clause is not present in

---

[15] Reiffenstuel, lib. III, tit. XLV, n. 2.

[16] S. C. Indulg. et Reliq., decr. Dec. 16, 1749—*Decr. Auth.*, n. 183; *Collectanea*, n. 375.

[17] Reiffenstuel, lib. III, tit. XLV, n. 27.

the documents issued by the Cardinal Vicar of Rome does not argue that relics authenticated by him may be exhibited without the local Ordinary's permission. Every relic publicly venerated must be approved by the local Ordinary, regardless of its former documents or attestations. The churches of exempt religious are not excused from the observance of this law, because the privilege of exemption does not carry with it the right to act independently of the Ordinary in those matters which affect the public devotions of the faithful, particularly in the cult of relics.[18]

The Ordinary may delegate this power of approving relics, but the Vicar General may neither approve nor authenticate unless with special permission of the Ordinary. This had been a rule with the Congregation of Relics for years, and it was sustained by Pius V.[19] Permission given to the Vicar General need not be written.

The approval of relics by the Ordinary is usually given in writing though this is not strictly necessary.[20] As a rule, it is done by appending to the document of authenticity some phrase of approbation. No set form is required, nor need the Latin language be necessarily used. Thus: *"It is permitted to expose these relics of Saint N."* or *"Expositio publica harum reliquiarum Sancti N.......permittitur,"* are licit formulae, provided that they are followed by the signature of the Ordinary (or his delegate), and the date of the month and year.

B. *Relics discovered not authentic to be removed from public cult.* There is something inherently unbecoming in the preservation of cult for a thing which is known to be spurious. Canon 1284 commands the abolition of all such devotions. Pius X put forth this law,[21] but it was not something new in the Church. Gratian had taken into his *Decretum* canon 50 of the Council of Africa, in 424, and this forbade the retention of altars without relics or with relics which were suspicious.[22] Pope Leo III

---

18 S. R. C., *Spoletana,* April 27, 1697—*Decr. Auth.,* n. 1971. Cf. also Ferraris, v. *Regulares,* art. II, n. 53.

19 S. C. Indulg. et Reliq., decretum, Sept. 23, 1780—*Decr. Auth.,* n. 240.

20 Mothon, *Institutions Canoniques,* II, n. 2498.

21 Litt. encycl., *"Pascendi,"* Sept. 8, 1907—*Acta Sanctae Sedis,* XL, 593; motu proprio, *"Sacrorum Antistitum,"* Sept. 1, 1910—*Acta Apostolicae Sedis,* II (1910), 664.

22 C. 26, D. I. *de consecratione.*

passed similar laws at the third Council of the Lateran in 1216. "Prelates are not to allow that persons who come into their churches to venerate and worship be deceived by false relics (figments or fragments), or by false documents, as has been done in many places for the sake of gaining filthy lucre." [23]

The Code is clear on this point: that all relics which are surely false must be removed from public cult. The obligation is chiefly incumbent upon the Ordinary, though it is not restricted to him, since other clerics are bound to see that there is nothing untrue in the devotion.

Customs that are immemorial may be allowed to continue, according to canon 5, if the Ordinaries think that they cannot prudently be abolished, on account of the circumstances of persons and places.[24] But nevertheless, this does not grant any justification for the maintenance of cult to a relic that is patently false. Unfounded beliefs and sentimental practises may heighten the devotions of some particularly fervent souls, and may, in fact, lead some individuals to greater heights of sanctity; but all such active or passive toleration of known frauds by ecclesiastical officials will inevitably discredit the Church and lead to derision and irreligion. Because some things were tolerated in times past, the Church has received wholesale abuse for the patronage of frauds, when the blame should have been placed upon officials who were negligent in their duties.

Mabillon had tried to justify some doubtful relics by the following argumentation:

> When there is solid doubt about the authenticity of any relic, one should not be influenced save by certain, clear and evident proofs to the contrary. Even when such proofs to the contrary are had, one ought to consider whether suppressing the relic would cause more harm and evil than tolerating it. Many relics are false, or exceedingly suspicious, but still their cult goes on. On the one hand, no one is forced to venerate the object; and on the other hand, it is very difficult at times to give a clear and conclusive

---

[23] C. 2, X, *de reliquiis et veneratione sanctorum,* III, 45.

[24] . . . Aliae (consuetudines), quae quidem centenariae sint et immemorabiles, tolerari poterunt, si Ordinarii pro locorum ac personarum adjunctis existiment eas prudenter submoveri non posse.

> proof that the relic is false. Old devotions are engrained in the hearts of the people, and sometimes their abolition would be difficult without commotion and scandal.[25]

This last point does not find complete critical approval. It might be expedient in some cases to permit an arrant error to continue temporarily rather than cause turmoil by denouncing and condemning it, but it is doubtful whether this policy of expediency produces more lasting fruits of good than of harm. The longer the Church permits the continuance of a devotion to a relic which is known to be a fraud or at least exceedingly suspicious, so much the more ridicule is heaped upon the Faith when the truth is finally known. Even to act passively in these affairs, by not condemning what is surely an abuse or an excess, is construed as a tacit approval and approbation of the practise.

Relics are not to be excluded and condemned on the mere basis of their improbability, or admitted because of their seeming probability, though such standards offer corroboratory proof for any decision in their regard.[26] The documents for each relic are to be examined carefully and completely. They must be signed, and stamped with the seal of the prelate who enclosed the relics in their container; and the container itself (or the reliquary) must have the relics enclosed and fastened within by silk cords, tied in such a way that the knot is imbedded in wax bearing the impressed stamp of the same prelate. The authenticating document describes the relic, and so a fair degree of certainty is possible in the matter of verification when the Ordinary who investigates is able to see that the relics are ". . . in a metal casket, of round shape, covered with glass and well enclosed, fastened with a red silk cord, and signed with our seal . . ." Caution must be used, however, even in the acceptation of these documents if the relics are supposed to have come from the Catacombs. If their documents have been issued

---

[25] *Lettre d'un Benedictin touchant le discernement des anciennes Reliques, au sujet d'une dissertation de M. Thiers contre la sainte Larme de Vendôme,* Paris, 1700.

[26] S. R. C., *Anagnina,* August 3, 1697—*Decr. Auth.,* n. 1977, where relics of the highpriest Melchisedech were rejected, as also were relics supposed to be part of the place where Christ stood when He composed the Lord's Prayer.

by the Cardinal Vicar of Rome, they may be assumed as authentic; if they bear letters of authenticity issued by any other prelate, even in Italy, they are to be questioned, because they are suspicious in their source. It may also be stated, as a general rule, that all relics supposedly from the Catacombs which made their appearance in the ten years between 1870 and 1880, or which bear a date within that time, are suspicious. No Ordinary should authenticate them or approve them for public cult.[27]

The Code tells the Ordinaries to act prudently in this matter of ending devotion to false relics. The law will be fulfilled if he acts quietly and slowly, without allowing any undue publicity to his movements, and without exciting commotion among the people. Augustine says that "Ordinaries would do well to withdraw and destroy relics which are certainly spurious." [28] This is not strict enough, since the Code makes the obligation compulsory, and not merely optional or discretionary. The *"prudenter amoveant"* is not merely advice, but a command. This conclusion must necessarily follow, especially since Pius X, in the *"Sacrorum Antistitum"* of 1910, enuntiated not merely a request but a command and a law.[29]

C. *Relics whose documents for authenticity have been lost.* In canon 1285, the Code makes provision for situations which arise when relics have lost their authenticating documents. All such relics are to be removed from public veneration, and are not to be exhibited again until the local Ordinary has made a new examination of them and has satisfied himself that they are genuine, just as their lost documents declared. The relics do not become false as soon as their "authentics" are lost, but nevertheless the Church demands that they be removed from public services until a new canonical approval and legal status be given them by the Ordinary. Here again, as in canon 1283, it is stated that the Vicar General may not act validly without a special mandate of the Ordinary. This implies that all authentication pertains primarily to the Ordinary.

---

[27] Vicariatus Urbis, litt. encycl., Jan. 17, 1881—*Collectanea,* n. 1546.

[28] *A Commentary,* VI, 250.

[29] Pius X, motu proprio, *"Sacrorum Antistitum,"* Sept. 1, 1910—*AAS,* II (1910), 664.

How is he to proceed in the examination of such relics? "Caute procedere debet Episcopus" is the common advice of all authors. Lehmkuhl says that he should not act unless he has the advice and counsel of theologians and other prudent men, so as to reach a verdict in conformity with truth and piety.[30] Craisson says the same,[31] and so also does Cocchi.[32] All of them are only repeating what the Council of Trent said, i.e., ". . . New relics are not to be received unless with the knowledge and approbation of the Bishop, who, as soon as such relics are presented to him, will take counsel with theologians and other pious men and reach a decision in conformity with truth and piety . . ."[33] Benedict XIV was more explicit and to the point when he stated that it was not necessary to have physical or metaphysical certitude in regard to the relics, since moral certitude sufficed,—both for judgments made by individual Bishops and by the Congregation of Rites. In case that relics are approved by Rome, however, more certainty is required because approbation there is of more import than any given by a bishop.[34] The testimony of one person is not sufficient to establish this moral certainty.[35] Mothon has the same indications as the others, but after counselling "une grande prudence" he adds that Ordinaries in all such cases may demand an oath from those who testify in favor of the authenticity.[36] The sworn testimony of one reputable person would seem to produce moral certainty in ordinary cases.

These are all good safeguards against the introduction of new relics into Church veneration. Whenever there are other historical, scientific or critical means of checking and verifying the relics, these also should be used. All documents, lists, charts,

---

[30] *Theologia Moralis*, II, n. 486.

[31] *Manuale Totius Juris Canonici*, I, n. 1027.

[32] *Commentarium*, III, n. 114—advising a thorough investigation of all the relic, the constancy of its traditional veneration, the testimony of pious persons, and all written proof possible to acquire.

[33] Conc. Trid., sess., XXV, *de invocatione, veneratione, et reliquiis sanctorum, et sacris imaginibus*.

[34] Benedict XIV, *De Beatificatione et Canonizatione Ss.*, lib. IV, pars 2, cap. 24, n. 9.

[35] *Ibidem*, c. 25, n. 1.

[36] Mothon, *Institutions Canoniques*, II, n. 2497.

monuments of whatsoever kind, capable of throwing light on the authenticity of the relics should be examined. Not only the documents should be scanned, but the relics themselves should be closely inspected. Ocular inspection is frequently the best way to acquire truth in this difficult matter. Thus Cardinal Paleotus summoned skilled anatomists to examine the remains of Sts. Vitalis and Agricola, and to testify whether all the characteristic marks of genuine relics were present. They tested the size of the remains, the odor, the color, the shape and all the other notes of distinction.

If the bishop has used all possible diligence and still is unable to demonstrate that relics are authentic, he is not to allow public exposition of them. If true and authentic relics are mingled with doubtful or uncertain relics, so that the true cannot be distinguished from the uncertain, the bishop ought to suppress devotion to all of them. Some theologians said that the true relics would sanctify the uncertain, just as unconsecrated oil is made sacred if mixed with consecrated oil. Relics, however, are not connected one with the other, and hence it would be better for the bishop to remove all from public veneration than to run the danger of approving a falsity.[37]

When a relic has in its favor not only antiquity but also official seals, signatures of officials and testimony, it will be very certain. Ancient parchment documents for authenticity which

---

[37] Honoratus a Sancta Maria [1651-1729], in two dissertations, published in *Réflexions sur les Règles et l'Usage de la Critique,* discussed at length the relics of Christ and the Passion, and the relics of the Saints. Both dissertations are masterpieces of scholarly and critical technique. *Réflexions sur les Règles* was published in three volumes, the first two at Paris in 1712 and 1717, and the third at Lyons in 1720. All three were later translated into Latin, Italian and Spanish. The Latin version was printed at Venice in 1840, and is titled *Animadversiones in Regulas et Usum Critices.* The dissertations on Relics are in the third tome, pp. 357-497.

The author formulated several rules to be used in determining the authenticity of relics. The principles of his system are apodictic and indisputable as far as they go, but they are not capable of an easy application to all cases. When they are applied to all relics of the past, they are capable of weeding out many falsities, but they are not so infallible as to be termed the basic principles of an exact science. They are good indications (as the author himself called them), but they are not infallible and easy tests by which all relics may be verified and authenticated.

have faded so much that the letters can not be deciphered may be accepted as genuine, provided that there is some way of knowing that they were formerly real letters of verification. A priest who had copied one such document before it faded completely had drawn up a document acceptable to prove the authenticity of the relics.[38]

The authenticating officials ought to examine the relics themselves and their closed containers with the wax-impressed seal that is found in all genuine relic-caskets of recent date. They should trace back the history of the relic to a time beyond the memory of men now alive, and try to ascertain whether there was ever any period in its history when its authenticity was denied by serious and trustworthy persons. If, after full investigation in this manner, all the characteristic marks of the relics bear testimony to the extreme likelihood and the moral certainty of its authenticity, new approval for it ought to be granted.[39]

D. *Ancient relics to be preserved in same veneration as formerly.* Relics that have been honored from time immemorial, i.e., "for many centuries"[40] are to be retained in the same veneration as formerly, unless they can be proved false by certain and incontrovertible evidence. The Code recognizes the impossibility of proving conclusively the objective truth of ancient relics, partly because of their antiquity and partly because of the lack of contemporary historical sources to corroborate their apparent genuineness. At the same time, the proving force in a long and well-established tradition cannot be rejected. If the people in some place have consistently honored a relic, and if there is nothing unbecoming in its cult, then the Code rules that the relic should be retained in its former status. These conditions being present, all the legal and moral presumptions favor its truth.

This policy is sound and justifiable, because it cuts midway

---

[38] Honoratus a S. Maria, *Animadversiones*, III, 480 ss.

[39] S. C. Indulg. et Reliq., *Divion.*, Feb. 22, 1847—*Decr. Auth.*, n. 335. Even though the relics are of Saints whose names are unknown, they may be venerated as *Relics of the Saints*, but no new names are to be assigned them except by the *Lipsanotheca*.

[40] Mothon, *Institutions Canoniques*, II, n. 2497.

between extreme rigor and excessive credulity. It would be just as wrong to condemn all ancient relics as false, as to canonize all as true. That being so, it is better—in the face of insuperable difficulties—to let the ordinary good practises go on, provided that they found some moral certainty that the relics in the first days of their cult were permitted and approved by the local bishops. That was the rule of action given by the Congregation of Relics and Indulgences on several occasions,[41] as well as by the Congregation of the Council.[42] It prescinds from the objective truth or falsity of the relics, though it presupposes them as authentic.

The Code does not say that new *documents* of authenticity are to be issued, but merely that there should be a "judgment of the Ordinary" concerning their verity, and that this judgment may not be made by the Vicar General except by special mandate of the Ordinary. Whether this *judgment* of the Ordinary should be written is not stated. The Code itself does not impose any obligation. It seems right, however, that it should be in writing, so that a legal and canonical status for the future will be imparted to the relic. Such a written judgment would assume the nature of an authentication and an approval, but its main feature would be that of an approval, based on the apparent truth of the relics and the liceity of permitting their cult to continue. Any brief formula will satisfy. Thus: *"It is permitted to expose these relics of Saint N."* would suffice, if signed and dated by the Ordinary or his delegate. Should the relics be examined and thus approved during the time of the episcopal visitation, the permission granted may be inserted in the official acts of visitation. This will suffice to grant a canonical basis for the future settlement of doubts which may arise.[43]

It is not beyond the bounds of possibility, however, that many ancient relics are spurious. What would be the result if, by errors made in good faith, these should be approved and publicly venerated? It would be a mistake, of course, but there

[41] S. C. Indulg. et Reliq., *Andegaven.*, Feb. 29, 1864 *Decr. Auth.*, n. 400; Iacen., Jan. 20, 1896—*Collectanea,* n. 1911.

[42] S. C. C., *Albiganen.*, March 14, 1648; *Albanen.*, March 3, 1668 ad *4um.*

[43] Craisson, *Manuale,* I, n. 913; Ferraris, v. *Visitare,* n. 95.

would not be anything disastrous in it. The material vestige of any relic is only the object around which the cult centres, and even though the relic should be false, the cult attains its real end, namely, the honor of the Saint.[44] A false relic of a Saint would not nullify or invalidate all the acts of devotion occasioned by it.

It must be repeated that the Church, in allowing the continuance of devotion to relics that have been honored since ancient times, does not state that they are true or genuine. The most that can be said is that the Church assumes their certainty rather than their falsity, because of the weight of the evidences in their favor. Even when apparently real miracles are wrought through them, the Church does not step in and declare that the relics are authentic, or proved genuine by the miracles.

> The correlation between the miracles and the authenticity of a relic is not presumed, but is regularly excluded by the way these things come to pass. . . . The miracles extoll only the goodness of God and the efficacy of prayer; and these two causes are independent of the authenticity of a relic. . . . Therefore we should, as a general rule, separate the pretended proof based on miracles from all controversy relative to the authenticity of a relic or to the truth of a historic fact. . . . The Church endeavors to protect the faithful from all error and superstition in the matter of relics, but She does not enjoy any infallibility or any privilege in these matters. The means which are employed to assure authenticity are the ordinary criteria which the world uses to verify historic facts. That is the limit of Her role and Her actions, and there Her responsibility ends. . .[45]

That has always been the attitude of the Church in allowing the continuance of ancient devotions, so long as no explicitly contradictory evidence has appeared. A prior right based on long-standing customs is better than a claim based on a probable opinion.[46]

---

[44] Perrone, *Praelectiones Theologicae*, II, p. 435, n. 105; Leibnitz, with testimony cited on page 24 as above; Delehaye, *Legends of the Saints*, p. 168.

[45] Chevalier, *Étude Critique sur l'Origine du sainte Suaire de Lirey-Chambéry-Turin*, p. 49.

[46] Pius X, litt. encycl., *"Pascendi,"* Sept. 8, 1907—*Acta Sanctae Sedis*, XL, 593; motu proprio, *"Sacrorum Antistitum,"* Sept. 1, 1910—*AAS*, II (1910), 664 ss.

The attitude and policy of the Church in permitting the cult of many ancient relics, particularly those of the Passion, is the same as the attitude toward the belief in private revelations or miraculous shrines. Perhaps no better illustration of the policy can be found than the Church approbations given to the Holy House of Loretto, which—tradition says—is the same house in which the Virgin Mary received the visit of the Angel Gabriel at the time of the Annuntiation. This is not merely a private place of devotion and pilgrimage, because it has received many approbations and favors from the Pontiffs of past ages.[47] Public devotions have been allowed and approved there by the Holy See because of the existence of a *tradition,* which apparently extends back as far as the actual time of the translation of the house into Italy by the angels. In the granting of favors and indulgences to that shrine, the Church and the Pontiffs did not commit the Church to the absolute and irrevocable stand that this tradition is true, nor did the letters of approbation entail any question of the Church's infallibility being called into court to establish or substantiate the truth of the popular beliefs. The main idea in the permission of a proper Mass and Office in honor of that shrine was the intention of doing honor to the Mother of God. The judgment that this really was the actual Holy House of Nazareth rested upon the evidences brought forth to corroborate the tradition. From the historical facts alleged in its favor, the Pontiffs had drawn conclusions that the traditions were worthy of belief and human faith, and hence were sufficient reasons for allowing public cult in that place. The letters of approval did not canonize or sanctify that house at Loretto, nor did they declare with finality that all the traditions about it were true. The Roman prelates had acted in a human fashion, taking their justification from the natural preponderance of evidence in favor of the place. As late as 1916, the Congregation of Rites has declared itself in favor of the House at Loretto, but even that does not settle the case. Always

[47] Paul II, on Feb. 12, 1470; Julius II, on Oct. 21, 1507. Cf. also S. R. C., *Lauretana,* May 9, 1606—*Decr. Auth.,* n. 210; *Aquen.,* Mar. 3, 1761—*Decr. Auth.,* n. 2461; *Lauretana,* Dec. 16, 1766—*Decr. Auth.,* n. 2483; *Ordinis Minorum,* July 2, 1897—*Decr. Auth.,* n. 3959.

there must be kept in mind the traditional policy of the Church in giving assent in such matters. This has been presented in the encyclical *"Pascendi"* of Pius X, where the Holy Father spoke first about private revelations and later applied all his previous words to relics.

> The Holy See neither approves nor denies these apparitions or revelations. It permits them to be believed with a purely human faith, resting upon the traditions that support them and receiving corroboration from the arguments and evidences which are worthy of credibility.
>
> Whoever holds this will have no fear, for the religious character of every apparition, in so far as it is called *relative* and regards the fact, always has the implicit condition that the fact is true; in so far as it is *absolute*, it is always based on truth, and is directed toward the person of the Saints who are honored. The same is to be said about Relics. . . .

Today, there are schools of Catholic authors who hold the contradictory views on the truth of the Holy House of Loretto, just as there are contradictory views on many other ancient relics. Both sides of the controversy cannot be correct, and one of them must be wrong. What is the position of Canon Law in such cases as these? What right have Church prelates to allow veneration for some thing, when many serious authors doubt the truth of it?

The traditional policy of the Church in conflicts such as these has been the most practical and sane solution of an apparently insoluble difficulty. Canon Law, which governs the external acts of the Church, has settled its conscience by the use of reflex principles. Wherever it is possible to acquire truth, then the truth and that alone will suffice;[48] but where it is impossible to burrow into history and establish the objective truth of a relic which lacks complete proof for authenticity, the Church has consistently retained devotions which are decent and worthy and honorable. There is justification for this stand, too, in the consideration that the Church is not a scientific laboratory with canonical test-tubes for determining the value of external cere-

[48] This is now expressed in canon 1284, which does not allow veneration of relics known to be false.

monies, but rather a college of souls and a society instituted for the spiritual good of the individual members. A false relic would not be an irritant element, capable of invalidating or nullifying all good acts occasioned by it. Relics are only means to devotion, not an end in themselves, and even though they should be fictitious, any person who honors them is performing an act of cult to the saints. The merit comes not from the object, but from good intention of the person.

What should be the policy, if the more common opinion agreed that the relic were false? First of all it must be remembered that it is exceedingly difficult to measure truths mathematically and to say when the numerical preponderance of experts on one side of the question outweighs those who hold opposite views. It has been the practise of prelates of the Church to allow continuance of devotion to relics whose authenticity is denied by some persons, so long as there is some solid probability that they are true. If the falsity is established conclusively and explicitly, the relic must be dropped from public cult, because the Church does not need forgeries or ignorance to promote religious devotions. "Hath God any need of your lie, that you should speak deceitfully for Him?"[49] If, however, there is a sufficiently serious reason which imparts solid probability to the ancient relic the Church has allowed its veneration. This is all the more true whenever there is public devotion founded on long-standing traditions. Until certain and conclusive proofs to the contrary are adduced, ancient relics may be retained in their former public veneration.[50] *Multorum devotio paucorum doctrinae cedere non debet,*—especially when the *doctrina paucorum* does not establish incontrovertible certainty. Vermeersch adds another reason why the Church allows continuance of devotion to ancient relics. Constant devotion before such things, and spiritual favors obtained through them can give them a sacred character and a title of honor distinct from their authenticity.[51]

Chevalier has unearthed documents regarding the early history of that famous relic known as the Sacred Shroud of Turin,

---

[49] Job, XIII, 7.
[50] Canon 1285 §2.
[51] *Epitome,* II, p. 329, n. 612.

and has presented strong proofs that the relic at Turin is not the real Shroud in which the Body of Christ was wrapped in the sepulchre. One of the documents is a brief of Clement V, issued on January 6, 1390, and it quotes the Pope as taking a unique attitude in regard to the famous relic. An early bishop had forbidden all priests to say anything about the Holy Shroud in their sermons to the people, and forbidden its exposition to the faithful under pain of excommunication. The case was appealed to Rome, and the Holy Father reversed all previous restrictions against the exposition of the Shroud and imposed *silentium perpetuum* on the bishop as regards such severe prohibitions. The Shroud could be exposed, he said, but the cleric who held it was commanded to say in a loud and intelligible voice that this thing was not the real Shroud, but only a picture or a representation of the authentic one.[52]

Here is a strikingly good instance of the Church attitude toward ancient relics. Their primary purpose is the furtherance of religion and religious practises. Their objective verity is not essential for true acts of devotion, and if they are fit and worthy, they can be used as representations or images of the saints, so long as they are not represented as being real or authentic.

It goes without saying that contradictory relics should never be authenticated or approved by any Ordinary. It does not require any profound erudition to agree with Mabillon maintaining that if there are two heads of St. John the Baptist, only one of them can be authentic. Toleration of such ridiculous extremes will be sure to earn opprobrium and derision for the whole Church, and any possible advantages which could follow from devotions to such contradictory relics would be completely outweighed by the ridiculous inconsistency of ecclesiastical officials. The exact procedure which must be followed by an Ordinary who has been asked to approve or authenticate a relic which another place already claims to have in its possession is not outlined in detail in any book of Church law or processes,—probably for the reason that the Holy See leaves the whole handling of such matters to the religious instincts of reverence

[52] Chevalier, *Étude Critique sur l'Origine du Saint Suaire,* Appendice K, p. xvi.

and tact in every Ordinary. Rather than authenticate or approve any such relic which contradicts one already in existence, the Ordinary ought to remit the whole case, with all its details, to the Congregation of Rites, since that is the proper forum for the settlement of all exceptional doubts of this nature. The jurisdiction formerly enjoyed by the Congregation for the care of Relics has now been committed to this part of the Roman Curia, ever since the constitution of Pius X in 1908.[53]

Ordinaries possessed the fullest powers in times past, conditioned only upon their unbiased judgments concerning the reliability of the relics and their fitness for public devotions. Not always was there seeming uniformity of practise, even in the decisions of the Congregation of Rites. A decision in 1696 advised the Ordinary to use his right to authenticate relics which lacked documents,[54] while another reply in 1892 barred from public veneration other relics, though they appeared to be in a somewhat similar condition.[55] The rule to follow was not always easily defined in the past, but the law of the Code simplifies all procedure by giving the Ordinary the right to approve or reject, after examination, any undocumented relic. This power must be used with caution, however, so that there will be no desecration of a true relic or veneration of a false one.

All writers are ready to admit that the authentication of any relic is a difficult task, especially when the relic is ancient. It remained for Barbier de Montault to advance claims and views which even his sincerest admirers hesitated to accept. As a student of archeology and antiquity, he published six articles in the *Revue de l'Art Chrétienne,* in order to present his reasons for attributing authenticity to relics of Saint Cecilia preserved at the Cathedral in Albi. He went so far as to say that the verification of relics has now become ". . . a precise science, after an experience of many centuries, with fixed principles, certain rules and a rigorous method. Thanks to this science, the study

---

[53] Apost. const. *"Sapienti Consilio,"* June 29, 1908—*AAS,* I (1909), 7 seq.

[54] S. R. C., *Augustae Praetoriae,* July 21, 1696—*Decr. Auth.,* n. 1946 ad 4.

[55] S. R. C., *Lauden.,* June 23, 1892—*Decr. Auth.,* n. 3779 ad 5.

of the sacred remains of those honored in the Church with public cult has become simple and easy."[56]

The name of this science was *Lipsanography,* a word derived from Greek roots of the words *relic* and *writing.* In essence, it is nothing more than a critical survey of the history of each relic, together with the examination and evaluation of the tradition in its favor. According to his theory, peaceful and uninterrupted possession for more than a thousand years makes a most decisive argument for the relic's authenticity,—and not merely an *a priori* indication or strong presumption but a real and valid *a posteriori* demonstration. He attempted to prove his statements by his researches on the relics of St. Cecilia, but unfortunately his arguments are not so convincing as to destroy all doubt. His science is far from being a precise one, with set principles and inviolable rules. What he expresses as an actuality was rather a hopeful wish of his own, purely mental and eminently desirable, but far from being a real thing. The Bollandists, with dignified disdain,[57] did not share the optimism in his claims for the new science. "More than one reader will find that unless he possesses the secrets of this new science in the same degree as Msgr. De. Montault, it will not always be easy to find proper orientation in such matters. In the present case (that of the relics of St. Cecilia) many difficulties will be encountered. . . . We cannot follow Msgr. De Montault in the lengthy development of his demonstration that the relics at Albi are authentic. Before we rally to the side of his proofs, we shall wait until the ingenious author has applied his proceedings to another group of relics, supposed to be those of the same saint,—in particular to the six different heads of the saint: two at Rome, and one each at Beauvois, Tours, Paris and Ouche. . . . Since Lipsanography has reached the state of an exact science, it is sure to reach an exact result . . ."

Barbier de Montault never accepted the challenge to prove his theory. Had he done so, he might have vindicated his cause and extended his researches so far as to present fixed rules by

[56] "Justification archéologique des Reliques de sainte Cecile, conservees autrefois et maintenant a la metropole d'Albi," 1894-1895.

[57] *Analecta Bollandiana,* XV (1896), 335.

which the validity of all relics could be tested and established. He would have done a great favor for the Church and for Canon Law, if he had been able to illustrate the certainty of his science in its ability to discover the truth of ancient and disputed relics. His enthusiasm, however, seemed to run ahead of stern reality, and his optimistic claims for Lipsanography were not seconded by any other writers, either during his time or after him.

In the year 1699, Jean Baptiste Thiers, a French cleric, had also outlined a plan for determining the authenticity of ancient relics, but it was so rigid that few, if any, relics could have been verified by it. According to Thiers' plan, relics had to be supported by some written document, or by divine, apostolic or ecclesiastical tradition which was constant, non-interrupted and continually manifested in the popular belief and practise since the first days of its possession. Mabillon admitted the utility of having such a well-supported tradition, but denied that it was necessary for the authentication of relics by any prelate. He was not unaware of the difficulty in the matter of verification, for he had seen too much of the Catacombs to ignore that. He recognized the stubborn fact that it was often impossible to know with physical certainty whether a relic venerated in some particular church was really and truly a relic of the person to whom it was ascribed. In the majority of situations, with physical certainty in the case impossible, a real moral certainty could be attained if careful consideration were paid to the external circumstances surrounding the relic and its devotion. Just as the Council of Carthage in 401 allowed the continuance of veneration to relics which had the favorable testimony of a *fidelissima traditio* so also did Mabillon recognize the proving force which long-standing and praiseworthy customs presented. These linked the present with the past, and were sufficient to justify the conclusion that any devotion which has produced such good fruits for centuries could not have been begun with error or fraud. He argued that in many cases it was just as impossible to prove that some thing *was not* an authentic relic as it was to demonstrate that it *was*. That being so, the balance of favor fell to the side of its authenticity whenever there was a long established custom of venerating it. He examined the rules which Thiers had set up for the discernment of true relics, and showed that they were untenable, false, unjust and impossible of application.[58]

The past is buried in the pages of history, and many of those pages are obscure and uncertain. Even the vicissitudes of the True Cross have been many and varied. Its fate is typical of the lot that has fallen to most ancient relics, because it has been sold, bartered in trade, burned, thrown into the ocean, carried in battle, captured by enemies, counterfeited, and transported into all parts of the civilized and uncivilized world. Much of the original Cross has been cut into small particles, and is now spread far and wide throughout the world. It has been the centre of fervent devotion, and the object of tremendous abuse. Erasmus, in days gone by, ridiculed the number of its relics, as did Macaulay in more recent times. Fulda has said that "there are enough of its relics to build a battleship." Calvin maintained that three hundred men could not carry all the relics of it that exist; Luther declared that there are enough of its relics to build a house; the American humorist Mark Twain remarked that there are enough of its relics to build a railroad across the Continent.

As a matter of fact, only a relatively small portion of the Cross can be accounted for. The stories of its immensity are absolute falsehoods. A survey has been made by Rohault De Fleury,[59] and not even one-tenth of the Cross has been discovered. Even though this survey was not scientifically thorough, it shows, nevertheless, that these relics were much fewer in num-

---

[58] Mabillon., *Lettre d'un Benedictin touchant le discernement des anciennes Reliques, au sujet d'une Dissertation de M. Thiers contre la Sainte Larme de Vendôme,* in fine. Cf. also Zallwein, *Principia Juris Ecclesiastici,* II, 149—"Regula Thierii in ordine ad demonstranda dogmata est bona; in ordine ad Reliquias probandas (est) pessima . . . falsa . . . injusta . . . temeraria. Regulae meliores sunt . . . traditio ecclesiastica . . . miracula vera et certa . . . revelatio . . . dyptica ecclesiastica . . . tituli, schedulae . . . judicium Episcopi." These remarks of Zallwein are all taken from Honoratus a Sancta Maria, *Animadversiones,* V, 480 ss.

[59] *Mémoire sur les Instruments de la Passion,* Paris, 1870. Cf. also Whitaker, "The True Cross," *The Sign,* VI (1927), 455 ff. for the present status of these relics. Halusa, "Kreuzreliquien," in *LQS,* LXXIV (1921), 52-59 covers the same matter.

ber than the exaggerated falsehoods assert. It is known that there were some forgeries and deceptions, but not on the wholesale scale that these stories maintain. Probably through some quirk in human nature, people will continue to believe these stories even after they have been revealed as falsehoods. They may not be true, but they are good stories. That is enough to ensure their longevity. Bellarmine traces many such wrong notions to the perverted histories written by the Magdeburg Centuriators.[60] De Combes also has a good point to make on this subject:

> ". . . Calvin had maliciously twitted Catholics with their many churches which claimed to possess the Title of the Cross [i.e., the Labarum, or the inscription 'Jesus of Nazareth, King of the Jews']. In fact, this multiplication of the Title furnished a standing joke to the Genevese reformer. Some good Catholics, with more faith than common sense had repeated the evasions of St. Paulinus of Nola and St. Cyril, and maintained that the Title was animated with a recuperative power which could replace anew every fragment torn from it. Bosio was better advised, and simply examined the Title. He was thus able to state, and this with truth, that Toulouse and other places had not the Title, but merely those parts of it not found at Santa-Croce. Toulouse, which Calvin had alleged as justification for his mockery, never claimed to possess more than a fragment of the Title. As such it was described by a deputation which examined it. . . . Other fragments are known to be kept at Rome . . . and at Agnani. That the Title was preserved entire in several places is thus shown to be a baseless fiction of the Calvinists . . ."[61]

What has been said about these relics of the cross may also be said about many other relics of antiquity. Seldom is it that there are written documents which date back to contemporary times. Most often there is only a tradition, more or less constant and uniform. With such pliable and elastic things as traditions to measure the verity of old relics, or at least to point out their authenticity, it is exceedingly difficult to put a finger upon the precise period at which fables or legends come to an

---

[60] *De Controversiis*, II, 463, "*De Reliquiis et Imaginibus Sanctorum.*"

[61] De Combes, *The Finding of the Cross*, pp. 188-89.

end, and truth begins. The Church has never held that the faithful were bound directly under pain or sin to believe in the authenticity of any ancient relic, of whatsoever kind or nature. It is possible that the Church official who issued the authenticating document was deceived. This is an accident liable to happen to any official charged with the issuance of public documents, because he must weigh the value of the assembled data, and judge whether there is moral certainty "beyond any reasonable doubt." The document for the authenticity of a relic, therefore, does not constitute it as authentic, but presupposes it as such. It is not a privilege or a dignity added to a relic; it is the statement of a verdict concerning it.

Manifestly, the only canonical rule that may be used in determining the authenticity of ancient relics is not a search for positive documentation or written attestations, but rather an impartial study of the history of each relic.[62] To the question, "Is this relic authentic?" the canonist must reply, "What is the history of the relic?" Canon Law is not History, or Epigraphy, or Archeology. It is the duty of these sciences to read and interpret the remains of past ages. Canon Law waits for the results of their investigations, accepts their verdicts, and is grateful for their assistance. If Archeology or Epigraphy can establish with certainty that some body disclosed is the actual remains of a real martyr, then Canon Law is grateful for the favor, and the relics are authenticated. If Archeology can bring no definite data, it is neither the province nor the scope of Canon Law to plunge into a field strange and foreign to its life and activity.

How, then, can Canon Law know whether ancient relics are true or false or suspicious? It must accept the testimony of the natural sciences, along with the stories that have come down in ancient traditions. In the past, the policy of the Church officials in the issuance of these authenticating documents was not always characterized by rigidity or severity. There always had to be a tradition in favor of the truth of the relic, but it is to be feared that many times some officials were not strict in exact-

[62] Honoratus a S. Maria, *Animadversiones,* V, 358 and 487. Mabillon, *Lettre d'un Benedictin,* had this point as a main objective.

ing requirements of constancy and non-interrupted continuance of popular belief. At times, they tolerated, by their non-condemnation, many relics which (in the common view today) should have been forbidden without delay. Such things have always been a source of embarrassment to Church historians. It seems preposterous and absurd that ecclesiastical toleration should have been granted to such relics as *lac beatae Mariae Virginis*, or to the tooth which Christ lost at the age of nine, or to the strands of hair which the Virgin Mother is supposed to have torn from her head while in anguish at the foot of the Cross.[63] Whether formal ecclesiastical sanction was ever granted to such relics as these is not known, but it cannot be denied, nevertheless, that certain localities claimed these relics, and were allowed to do so—unhindered for a time by any prohibitions of bishops or superiors.

These errors, however, were in ancient times, and ever since the Council of Trent centered in the local bishops the responsibility for local customs and stories, the abuses have for the most part died away. The inherent unfitness of a relic, or the apparent improbability of its truth, or the lack of ancient traditions to bolster its claims were some of the reasons used by the bishops in killing off many abuses, with the result that comparatively few of the ancient relics of extraordinary character survive at the present time. Barred from public devotions, they have passed into oblivion, ". . . unwept, unhonored, and unsung."[64]

E. *Vain controversies on authenticity of relics to be forbidden.* Enough has been said about the authenticity of relics to show that it is a difficult thing to establish. It would be easy to create more difficulties, because as a general rule, the more ancient a relic is, the less is known about its sources. This is true about all other ancient things, as well as about relics. Local Ordinaries, therefore, are told not to allow any discussions concerning the authenticity of ancient relics unless there is certainty

---

[63] Guibert, *De Sanctis et eorum Pignoribus, MPL,* CLVI, 649.

[64] Zallwein, *Principia Juris Ecclesiastici,* II, 153—showing that the centralization of power in the bishops made for a more canonical devotion. Thurston, "Relics," *Cath. Encycl.,* XII, 736 indicates that many relics at Rome were suppressed in this way.

in the proofs alleged. Any prejudiced arguments that rest upon mere conjectures or probabilities are not to be allowed a public hearing, when they are liable to undermine the popular religious beliefs of the people. Any publication of such denials, and other methods of procedure that will only cause ridicule and disdain for relics, are to be prohibited by the Ordinaries. The Code does not say which Ordinary has the prior obligation,—the Ordinary of the place where the relics are kept, or the Ordinary of the place where the discussions commence,—but the meaning of the law is clear from the purpose of the canon. That Ordinary who has the right and the duty to approve matter for publication is meant primarily, and it is his duty to censor all criticisms affecting the status of relics, even when the relics are outside his own jurisdiction.

This does not mean that once a relic is authenticated, it stands as authenticated forever, placed outside all possibility of doubt and scrutiny. It may and does happen that new evidences are brought to light which cast serious doubt upon the genuineness of particular relics. The obvious place to air those difficulties and to settle those doubts is not the diocesan newspaper or any magazine dedicated to the furtherance of religious piety and devotion. Neither is the Catholic pulpit the fit place to attack the authenticity of any relic.

Some of the provisions of this canon are taken from the encyclical *"Pascendi"* of 1907 and the motu proprio *"Sacrorum Antistitum"* of 1910,[65] while others are new in expression but old in practice. Sound and sober criticism of relics is not forbidden, provided that it be based on substantial evidences and provided also that it be done without turmoil in the devotional practices of the faithful. If it should be necessary to question the verity of some relics, this ought to be done with a view to establish the objective truth, respectfully and disinterestedly, and not with the spirit of mistaken broadmindedness that gleefully points out the errors of the past, as if to rejoice or to have others rejoice in the misfortunes that the Church has suffered because of the mistakes of some of Her members.

Augustine says that the prohibition of all such discussions is

---

[65] Pius X, motu proprio, Sept. 1, 1910—*AAS,* II (1910), 664.

not too strict, because the law of the Code ". . . leaves a large margin for solid arguments. The Bollandists [who edited critical Lives of the Saints] cannot be seriously accused of making exaggerated or unfounded statements."[66] Vermeersch distinguishes different kinds of criticism, allowing that which is sound and learned, and condemning that which is scoffing or contemptuous or ridiculing.[67] Prümmer also condemns these "hypercritical" attacks.[68]

In critical reviews or scientific essays, it is allowed to present conclusions which are contrary to commonly-accepted belief in particular relics, but it is never allowed to do this in magazines or periodicals that are intended for pious reading. The anxiety to show the falsity of one or many relics would not justify an author in breaking down, even unintentionally, the fundamental reverence for the whole cult.

The Church holds no briefs for the truth of any particular relics. When necessary conditions are fulfilled, the Ordinaries may authenticate them. That authentication is not infallible, nor is it pretended to be. Assent to the truth of an authentication is demanded and controlled by the ordinary faith in authority and the absence of prejudices. If contrary facts, sane and sound, are discovered by any person, he has the right to repudiate the pretended veracity of the relic; in the meantime, however, the traditional respect is to be given it.

The Code law in this canon is profoundly wise and learned. The Bollandists themselves have confessed the inability and the impossibility of penetrating all the ancient secrets of the past, even with the aid of all available manuscripts.[69] In the face of these insurmountable difficulties, it is right to let honorable and fitting devotions survive, especially when they are occasioning many religious acts of prayer and penance. If learned savants can bring scientific proof of their falsity, the Ordinary is told to

---

[66] *A Commentary,* VII, 251.

[67] *Epitome,* II, n. 613, note 1.

[68] *Epitome Juris Canonici,* p. 474, q. 392.

[69] *Analecta Bollandiana,* XIX (1900), 46-47, on the relic of the Blood of Our Lord; Delehaye, "Le Temoignage des Martyrologes," XXVI (1907), pp. 78-99.

remove the relics from public cult.[70] Until clear and incontestable proofs are offered, however, the Ordinary may allow them to continue. This is both legal and prudential.[71]

[70] Canon 1284—Locorum Ordinarii reliquiam quam certo non esse authenticam norint, a fidelium cultu prudenter amoveant.

[71] Motu proprio, *"Sacrorum Antistitum,"* Sept. 1, 1910, n. VI—*AAS,* II (1910), 664.

CHAPTER V

ART. 1. THE EXPOSITION OF RELICS

Canon 1287 §1. Reliquiae, cum exponuntur, in thecis seu capsis clausae et obsignatae sint oportet.

§2. Reliquiae sanctissimae Crucis nunquam in eadem theca cum reliquiis Sanctorum publicae venerationi exhibeantur, sed propriam thecam separatam habeant.

§3. Beatorum reliquiae, sine peculiari indulto, in processionibus ne circumferantur, neve in ecclesiis exponantur, nisi ubi eorum officium et Missa celebretur ex Sedis Apostolicae concessione.

A. *Relics publicly exposed to be enclosed and sealed in containers.* Relics destined for public veneration should be constantly enclosed in some capse (or reliquary), and securely attached within it by the waxen seal of the prelate who authenticated them for public cult. This law, made by Innocent III in 1216,[1] was incorporated by Gregory IX into his Decretals,[2] confirmed and reaffirmed by many other particular laws,[3] and remains in the new Code of Canon Law. Its motive is to prevent all profanation to relics and to secure for them more respect.

Relics are exposed and exhibited in small caskets or cases of varying shape and design,—some resembling a monstrance or glass-covered pyx, while others are in a box or frame with a glass-covered top through which the contents are visible. The

[1] IV Lateran Council, tit. 62, "*Ne Reliquiae Sanctorum exponantur extra capsam* . . ."—Mansi, XXII, 1050.

[2] C. 2, X, *de reliquiis et veneratione Sanctorum*, III, 45.

[3] Council I of Milan, in 1565, tit. 9—Mansi, XXXIVa, 44; Provincial Council of Bourges, in 1584, tit. 10, can. 2,—Mansi, XXXIVa, 888; Synod of Constance in 1300, tit. 19,—Mansi, XXV, 34; Synod of Bayeux, in 1300, tit. 40,—Mansi, XXV, 62.

authenticating documents describe the reliquary, usually in such words as these: "*. . . a silver theca, in the form of a cross (or of oval form), well-enclosed, fastened within by a red silk cord, and signed with our seal. . . .*" The reliquaries are often constructed in such a way that the *lipsanotheca* (or that small box containing the actual relics) may be lifted out and removed, but always the relics themselves cannot be touched or handled unless the red silk cord or the seal of the prelate be broken. When these latter are intact, one may be assured that the relics are in the same status as at the time of their authentication; but if either the seal or the silk cord fastening them within the container is broken, the relics may be considered as suspicious, and—apart from special circumstances where the possessor knows that the injury was done to the cord or the seal by some mishap[4]—must not be venerated in public devotions until the Ordinary has investigated them and declared in their favor by a new approval according to Canon 1285.

If the document for authenticity should be lost or destroyed, the relics are not to be exposed publicly until another approval of them has been issued. The original prelate who authenticated should be petitioned for another document. It may also be necessary to return the relics themselves to him for another inspection, unless the possessor knows and tells the number which was affixed to the document. If recourse would entail a long time and involved procedure, it seems that the local Ordinary may issue a letter of temporary approbation, provided that he has moral certitude about the truth of the relics. This will take the form of a permission allowing the relics to remain in public veneration, pending the arrival of the new authentication.

If the relics or the reliquaries appear to have been tampered with, the Ordinary should use every possible means to determine their genuineness.[5] In case of doubt persisting, he should order that they be given a quiet burial in consecrated ground; but in case he acquires moral certainty of their authenticity, he should

---

[4] Mothon, *Institutions Canoniques,* II, 453, n. 2497. ". . . S'il arrive que . . . les scellés, les cordons, ou le verre d ureliquiare soient brisés, en un mot, que le reliquiare ait pu être ouvert, il faut aussitôt, faire renouveler le document, ou remettre le reliquiare dans l'état où il doit être."

[5] Herdt, *Sacrae Liturgiae Praxis,* II, n. 192.

replace them in the reliquary, affixing both his own seal and that of the former prelate, which is already in the capse.

Sometimes it may be desirable to transfer relics from an old casket to another more fitting reliquary. "If it is sufficient to clean merely the outside of the old casket and transfer it bodily into the new case, this operation need not disturb the seal, and presents no difficulty. But if it is necessary to open the old casket and thus tamper with the seal, the latter should, of course, be re-affixed to the new case, and this could not be done without consulting the bishop to whom it belongs to see that the relics are properly preserved."[6]

When relics are not offered to exposition in a church, they should be kept (together with the documents of authentication and approval) in a secure place, under lock and key. No set place is determined for them by law. Morrisroe suggests as appropriate ". . . an arrangement by which they are located in a niche in the wall of the church or sacristy, fitted with a glass panel through which they may be viewed."[7]

B. *Relics of the True Cross to be separated from other relics of Saints.* Relics of the Cross or of the Passion are of a higher class than ordinary relics of the Saints, and the Church has insisted that they be separated and given special and distinctive honor. They must never be exposed for public veneration in any reliquary which contains at the same time relics of the Saints.[8] This prohibition does not affect relics used only for private veneration, however, since it relates only to public devotions. If reliquaries are not exhibited for public cult, the practice of keeping relics of the Saints and of the Cross together is not forbidden.[9] The same decrees which forbid the mingling of relics of the Cross with other relics of Saints demand the same observ-

[6] P. Morrisroe, "Custody and Veneration of Relics," *Irish Ecclesiastical Record,* XXII (1907), 536-537.

[7] Ibidem.

[8] S. C. Reliq., *Cenomanen.,* Feb. 22, 1847—*Decr. Auth.,* n. 342; S. R. C., decretum generale, May 27, 1826—*Decr. Auth.,* n. 2647; *Cenomanen,* Feb. 18, 1843—*Decr. Auth.,* n. 2854; *Bergomen.,* May 25, 1906—*Decr. Auth.,* n. 4186.

[9] Mothon, *Institutions Canoniques,* II, p. 460, n. 2505; Gennari, *Monitore Ecclesiastico,* XVI, 537.

ances for other relics of the Passion, such as parts of the Crown of Thorns.

The distinctive honors that must be paid to relics of the Passion are outlined in the Appendix. In this place, it is sufficient to state a few of the rules. After relics of the Cross or of the Passion have been exposed or carried in procession, blessing of the people with the relic *must* be given by the officiating minister;[10] but after exposition or procession with the relics of the Saints, the benediction *may* be given, though there is no obligation.[11] The priest stands and does not kneel when incensing the relics of the Passion.[12] Relics are not to be placed on the top of the Tabernacle, thus making it serve as a base. They are never to be exposed in front of the door of the Tabernacle, even on the great feast days. All contrary customs are abuses, and are condemned. The Congregation of Rites was strict on this matter, and stated that relics were not to be exposed for veneration at the altar of the Blessed Sacrament but at some other altar. If there is only one altar in a church, and if there is no other place to expose relics than above the Tabernacle, then the exposition ought to be entirely omitted. It is better to omit all, rather than do what is unbecoming. Even relics of the Cross come under this rule.[13]

C. *Restrictions on veneration for Relics of the Beatified.* Public exposition or veneration for the relics of persons who are Beatified or Blessed is allowed only in those churches which have received from the Holy See the right to say their Mass and Office.[14] Only in these same churches may the relics be carried in procession, on condition that a special and separate permission for the procession has been granted in an indult of the Holy See.[15] These indults come from the Holy See through the Con-

[10] S. R. C., *Brixien.*, Sept. 15, 1736—*Decr. Auth.*, n. 2324; *Dubiorum*, May 31, 1817—*Decr. Auth.*, n. 2578 ad 11 with the *Adnotationes Super Decreto 2578*, in *Decr. Auth.*, volume IV, page 162.

[11] *Adnotationes Super Decreto 2578, ut supra.*

[12] S. R. C., *Brixien.*, Sept. 15, 1736—*Decr. Auth.*, n. 2324.

[13] S. R. C., *Decreta Authentica*, IV, 203—*Suffragium* with commentary on decrees 2613 ad 6, 2740 ad 1, 2906; DeHerdt, *Sacrae Liturgiae Praxis*, II, n. 199.

[14] S. R. C., decl., April 17, 1660—*Decr. Auth.*, n. 1156 ad 4.

[15] S. R. C., decretum super cultu Beatis adhuc non Canonizatis praestando, Sept. 27, 1659—*Decr. Auth.*, n. 1130 ad 11.

gregation of Rites, and the privileges they confer are not communicable to other churches.

ART. 2. RELICS IN THE PECTORAL CROSS OF A BISHOP

Canon 1288. Sanctissimae Crucis reliquiae, quas in cruce pectorali Episcopus forte defert, ecclesiae cathedrali, ipso defuncto, cedunt, Episcopo successori transmittendae; et si defunctus pluribus praefuerit dioecesibus, ecclesiae cathedrali dioecesis, in cuius territorio supremum diem obiit aut, si extra dioecesim mortuus est, ex qua ultimo discessit.

Acting at the command of Leo XIII in the year 1889, the Cardinal Vicar of Rome sent an encyclical letter to all the Bishops of the world, concerning the relics of the True Cross which many possessed and retained in their pectoral crosses. The Pontiff saw that these relics were becoming more rare as time went on, and wishing to make sure that future bishops would be able to acquire some of these precious particles for their own crosses, he earnestly recommended that all such relics should be transmitted to the successors of deceased Bishops, under the legitimate title of heredity.[16] In this way, future new Bishops would be spared the arduous task of trying to secure some of these rapidly diminishing relics, since there is one of them attached to their office as the "proper mark of their dignity."[17]

The suggestion of that Pontiff has become a law in the Code, and the interpretation of that law must follow the plan set down in the former encyclical letter. Accordingly, canon 1288 does not demand that all other relics which may be in the pectoral cross are to be transmitted to the successor of a deceased Bishop, but only those of the True Cross. Neither is there any obligation to transmit the pectoral cross itself, or the reliquary. These latter have a pecuniary value, and—after the relics have been removed—may be freely given away, or left in legacy to one's heirs, or even sold. There should not be any unseemly or unbe-

---

[16] Vicariatus Urbis, litt. encycl., March 25, 1889—*Collectanea*, n. 1699. Cf. also *American Ecclesiastical Review*, I (1889), 468.

[17] *Loc. cit.*, ". . . veluti proprium suae dignitatis gestamen . . ."

coming negotiation, however,[18] in accord with the traditional reverence of the Church for all things once dedicated to a holy purpose. If the pectoral cross should be sold, it will lose all the blessing or consecration which may have been attached to it.[19]

Canon 1288 also provides for exceptional cases where the deceased Bishop happens to be the Ordinary of several dioceses. In whatever one of his dioceses he dies, to that diocese belongs the relic; if he should die outside the territory of his dioceses, the title to the relic reverts to that diocese of his jurisdiction which he had most recently left.[20]

The duty of preserving the relic for the rightful successor of the dead Bishop will rest upon the Cathedral chapter, or upon the person or persons who take the place of the Bishop when the see is vacant.[21] In the United States, therefore, this duty would devolve upon the diocesan concultors and the Administrator, according to the common law for the Church in this country.[22]

---

[18] Loc. cit., ". . . remota quavis indecorae aut profanae negotiationis specie . . ."

[19] Cf. *Rituale Romanum, Appendix, Benedicenda ab Episcopo,* n. III—for the blessing of a reliquiary. It is reserved to a Bishop but may be delegated by him to another.

[20] Augustine, *A Commentary,* VII, 252 (edition of 1921) makes it seem that the relic, in the latter case, would belong to the cathedral church of the place where he died. The Code is contrary to that.

[21] Vicariatus Urbis, litt. encycl., March 25, 1889—*Collectanea,* n. 1699.

[22] Canons 423—444 relate the powers and duties of the diocesan consultors during the life and after the death of the Ordinary. They have the same powers as the cathedral chapter, and may elect an Administrator within eight days from notification of the Bishop's death. This Administrator has the duty of safeguarding the relics in the cross.

CHAPTER VI

SALE OF RELICS IS FORBIDDEN

Canon 1289 §1. Sacras reliquias vendere nefas est; adeoque Ordinarii locorum, vicarii foranei, parochi aliive curam animarum habentes, sedulo caveant ne sacrae reliquiae, praesertim sanctissimae Crucis, occasione maxime hereditatum aut alienationis acervi bonorum, veneant, neve in acatholicorum manus transeant.

§2. Rectores ecclesiarum, ceterique ad quos spectat, sedulo invigilent ne sacrae reliquiae ullo modo profanentur, neve hominum incuria pereant, vel minus decenter custodiantur.

A. *Precautions against sale of Relics.* Simony is defined as "the sedulous attempt to buy or sell for a temporal advantage something that is spiritual, or which is annexed to what is spiritual."[1] It is a sin against religion, and it partakes of the nature of a sacrilege, since it is the evaluation of a spiritual thing in terms of the material. The sale of sacred relics of the Saints or the Beatified has always been forbidden by the Church, because it is simony.

Cocchi maintains that all sale of relics is simony *juris divini*, and his opinion seems right. It is impossible to divest relics of their sacred character, and the positive law in canon 1289 §1 is only the restatement of the divine law which forbids the sale of such objects.[2] Noldin, however, says that the ordinary sale would be only simony *juris ecclesiastici*, whether the relics are enclosed within a reliquary or are apart from one.[3] Ferreres

[1] Canon 727. This definition in the Code follows that set up by Saint Thomas, *Commentarium in Sententias*, IV, dist. 25, art. 1.

[2] *Commentarium*, III, 216.

[3] *Theologia Moralis*, II, n. 184.

states that the sale of a reliquary with relics enclosed would not even be simony *juris ecclesiastici,* if the price is based only upon the material value of the container and not upon the spiritual character of the contents. In such a case, the relics are considered as a free donation.[4] There is no law forbidding the sale of *reliquaries* alone, but Noldin states that their sale is forbidden if they have relics enclosed. This does not seem to be present in canon 1289, except by an extension of the law which demands reverence for all relics. Apart from a positive prohibition of the Church which might forbid such sales because of the appearance of relic-traffic, the sale of a reliquary that has relics within does not seem forbidden, so long as there is no scandal or bad intent present.

The law in the Code against the sale of relics comes from Innocent III, who formulated into positive legislation all the prohibitions coming from the natural and human laws.[5] His law remains in force today, because it protects the sacredness of the remains of Saints.

The purchase of relics from persons who would otherwise desecrate them is not simony, because the price paid is not solely for the sacred thing but for the prevention of their dishonoring, as well.[6] Nevertheless the buying of such relics on personal initiative is forbidden.[7] When relics are discovered offered for sale, the local Ordinary should be informed of the conditions, and it is his duty to take all possible means to stop the sale and to acquire the relics. If there should not be sufficient time to consult the Ordinary, and if the relics are in imminent danger of profanation, Genicot and others say that the law forbidding the purchase of relics will cease, because its very purpose (which is the recovery of the relics) will be defeated if its precepts are strictly observed.[8] This opinion seems justifiable, but it must

---

[4] *Compendium Theologiae Moralis,* I, n. 382-2°.

[5] C. 2, X, *de reliquiis et veneratione sanctorum,* III, 45.

[6] Genicot, *Theol. Mor.,* I, n. 288—V; Cocchi, *Commentarium,* III, 216; Vermeersch-Creusen, *Epitome,* II, n. 9.

[7] S. C. Indulg. et Reliq., decr., Dec. 21, 1878—*Collectanea,* n. 1506; Vicariatus Urbis, litt. encycl., Jan. 17, 1881—*Collectanea,* n. 1546.

[8] Genicot, *loc. cit.;* Cocchi, *loc. cit.;* Vermeersch-Creusen, *loc. cit.;* and Ballerini-Palmieri, *Theol. Mor.,* II, n. 475.

be used cautiously. Too often in the past has the willingness to pay money in exchange for relics resulted in the appearance of a plethora of them for sale. Before following this opinion, a person should have certainty that more good than evil will follow from his act.

B. *Relics not to be allowed to non-Catholics.* Local Ordinaries, rural deans, pastors and all others with the care of souls are commanded to protect relics, and to see that they do not become the property of non-Catholics. This last injunction is not a completely new law, for it had been formulated in two decrees of the Congregation of the Holy Office, one of which explained the other. By a decree of 1749, missionaries had been allowed to visit dying infidels, to recite prayers over them for enlightenment of mind and health of body, and to leave with such persons small religious articles, on condition that they would be kept with reverence. When asked in 1768 whether missionaries could leave relics of the Saints with such dying persons, the Congregation answered in the negative.[9]

The Code follows the same line of procedure, and forbids relics to all non-Catholics, whether heretics or infidels. The exclusion of Protestants from the right to possess them is not dictated by any organized hatred for them, but rather by the legal presumption that if non-Catholics follow the principles of their spiritual guides and leaders, they will have no respect for any relics at all. There would always be danger of desecration, if not at the present time (in the hands of a person well-disposed), then in the future (in the hands of another not favorable to the devotion). The cult of relics is a Catholic practice for Catholic people, and the privilege of possessing relics should not be allowed to those who are not Catholic at heart.

C. *Duty of authorities to prevent loss or desecration.* In many cases it will be impossible to prevent relics from passing into alien hands. This is a sad reality, evident from the fact that there is hardly a large museum in America which has not a quantity of relics of the Saints, sometimes with written documents for their authenticity. Some of them have relics of the

[9] S. C. C. Officii, instr., Dec. 11, 1749—*Collectanea,* n. 374; (Scopiae), August 11, 1768—*Collectanea,* n. 468.

True Cross. Surely, no Catholic can sell a first-class relic (or a reliquary containing such a relic) to any institution like that without incurring serious moral culpability. Canon 1289 is explicit in forbidding such transactions. Relics are sacred things, and their proper place is not a museum—for the stares of curiosity-seekers—but in sacred surroundings, or in a place that is calculated to inspire acts of religious devotion. Whenever there are relics in such improper places, the Ordinaries should make every effort possible to regain them for the Church. Rectors of churches and other persons with similar public offices are urged to be vigilant lest sacred relics be profaned in any way. They should not allow relics to be destroyed through the carelessness of their owners or the malice of men.[10] They should be ready to crush out superstition and unfit devotions, as well as prepared to guard against irreverent handling of the sacred particles. The virtue of the devotion does not lie in the excess or in the defect, but in the circumspect middle path of honor and reverence.

Benedict XIV stated that there was an excommunication *latae sententiae* incurred by those who took money in return for relics from the Roman Catacombs, or for the writing and issuance of documents or seals in favor of those relics. Even money freely offered could not be accepted, when occasioned by the transfer or donation of relics.[11] The penalty does not exist in the new Code, but the spirit of the law is the same. In the distribution of relics, it is right that a fit sum of money be given to compensate for the cost of the reliquary, since this is generally ornate or well embellished. But should the relic and reliquary be sold for an exorbitant price, far above the actual value of the relic-casket itself, such a transaction would be certain simony. No kind of sophistic reasoning could take the malice out of it, because it is nothing more than making relics of the Saints a direct means of pecuniary profit. Every law of the cult cries out against this.

D. *Penal sanction against dissemination of false relics.*

---

[10] *Ceremoniale Episcoporum,* l. I, c. VI, n. 2.

[11] *De Beatif. et Canoniz. Ss.,* lib. IV, pars 2, cap. 28, n. 10.

Canon 2326. Qui falsas reliquias conficit, aut scienter vendit, distribuit vel publicae fidelium venerationi exponit, ipso facto excommunicationem Ordinario reservatam contrahit.

A new penal sanction against the making or distribution of false relics has been added in the Code. Whoever makes false relics, or knowingly sells, distributes or exposes them to public veneration incurs *ipso facto* excommunication reserved to the Ordinary. The canon is directed only against false relics, without imposing any censure upon those who might perchance traffic in authentic relics.

Forgerers of false relics are those who so arrange bodies or parts of bodies (not of Saints) and so corroborate them with fictitious signs of authenticity that they are esteemed and honored as genuine by the faithful.[12] The actual deception of the faithful, however, does not seem to be required for the incurring of the censure. The bad will of a person with such dangerous tendencies is punishable, and even crass or supine ignorance of the law or censure will not excuse from censure those who forge false relics.[13] If the ignorance is less culpable than crass or supine (which is quite improbable to suppose) the Ordinary may inflict vindicative penalties, since the censure is not incurred by the guilty party.

The Code is less strict with those who sell, distribute, or expose false relics to public exposition than toward those other persons who manufacture the same, since the law states that crass ignorance excuses the former, but not the latter. The element of knowledge and advertence required for the incurring of the censure will often be lacking in persons who sell, distribute or publicly expose false relics. If there is any ignorance of fact (i.e., not knowing that they are false) or of the law (i.e., not

---

[12] Sole, *De Delictis et Poenis*, p. 254, n. 349.

[13] Canon 2229 3-1°, si lex verba illa [*scienter, studiose, consulto*, etc.] non habeat: 1° Ignorantia legis aut etiam solius poenae, si fuerit crassa vel supina, a nulla poena latae sententiae eximit; si non fuerit crassa vel supina, excusat a medicinalibus, non autem a vindicativis latae sententiae poenis. . . .

knowing that there is a censure attached to these acts), the censure is not incurred.[14]

If the sale is wilful and intentional, there is a censure regardless of whether it is done publicly or privately, and whether few or many relics are sold. Both lay persons and clerics may incur censure for the distribution of false relics, provided that the giver insinuates their genuineness while aware of their falsity. Even though they are given by a free donation, there is a censure incurred, because the purpose of the law is to prevent every act of cult for spurious things.

Both public and private veneration or exposition of such things are forbidden, because of their unfitness. Nevertheless, ". . . the exposing of false relics to *private* veneration is not punished with a censure,"[15] although it is surely forbidden. The Code has in mind the *public* exposition of such relics, and forbids this under pain of censure *latae sententiae.* The common opinion seems to be that only a cleric may fall under this censure for exposing false relics to public veneration, since no lay person is a subject legally capable of exercising ministerial powers in ecclesiastical ceremonies.[16]

This is a lenient interpretation, however, and it is based on the narrowest sense of the words in the law. The intention of the Code is clearly to quash all false relics and to punish all persons who presume to extend the life of forgeries. Half of the motive in this law is nullified if only clerics are affected by it. Noldin implicitly admits the possibility of a lay person incurring the censure, when he excuses a sacristan from the censure in a given case, not through the inability to incur it but rather because of grave fear of the pastor.[17]

In the absence of certainty, however, the favorable opinion may be followed, because this is penal legislation, and *odiosa sunt restringenda.* A lay person who knowingly deceived a priest into exposing false relics would not incur the censure by reason

---

[14] Sole, *De Delictis et Poenis,* p. 254, n. 350.

[15] Noldin-Schönegger, *De Censuris,* n. 88.

[16] Cerato, *Censurae Vigentes,* n. 70; Sole, *De Delictis,* n. 350; Vermeersch-Creusen, *Epitome,* III, n. 526; Capello, *De Censuris,* n. 375; Noldin-Schöenegger, *De Censuris,* n. 88.

[17] Noldin-Schonegger, *De Censuris,* n. 88.

of the public exposition, but he would incur it if he had sold such things to the priest, or distributed them while aware of their fraudulent character.

Exposition of relics whose documents for authenticity have been lost is not punished by the censure, since the relics are genuine. Nevertheless such exposition is forbidden by canon 1285.[18] Exposing relics whose authenticity is doubtful is not punished by the censure, though it is forbidden by the same canon.[19]

The sale of a false relic would not be simony, because the thing has no real sacred character, but nevertheless such sales or distributions are forbidden because they imply the possibility or the actuality of a false and erroneous cult.

---

[18] Cf. page 82.

[19] Canon 1285 §2, as on page 84.

CHAPTER VII

APPENDIX

Foreword

This appendix does not contain all the liturgical regulations for the cult of relics, but merely the most important canonical rules governing their use in public devotions. All books of Liturgy have the ceremonies outlined in detail. In this chapter there are four articles. The first has the regulations concerning relics in altars; the second tells the privileges of churches that possess a notable relic; the third describes the way in which relics should be preserved; the fourth outlines the rules for the exposition of relics, with particular comment on the place of exposition, the actual veneration by the faithful, the incensing by the priest, processions with relics, and finally the benediction given with them.

ART. 1. RELICS IN ALTARS

There is no direct or necessary connection between the Sacrifice of the Mass and the veneration of relics, but nevertheless the practice of depositing relics of the Saints beneath altars is very ancient, because of the Catholic belief that the martyrs deserve places of distinct honor in the churches. St. Augustine in North Africa had erected an altar over the relics of St. Stephen,[1] and spoke of another that had been erected over the relics of St. Cyprian.[2]

The fifth Council of Carthage in 401 condemned abuses where altars had been erected because of inane dreams of private revelations, without any relics of martyrs interred therein; but Braun warns against overestimating the value of this decree, because

[1] *Sermo 318, De Martyre Stephano, MPL,* XXXVIII, 1437.

[2] *Sermo* 313, *in Natali Cypriani Martyris,* V, 5, *MPL,* XXXVIII, 1413.

the law was made to legislate against abuses, and not to regulate or legislate concerning altars.[3] "There is no question at all of [this being] a decree which requires the placing of relics in the altar at its consecration."[4]

But if there were no general laws, there surely were general customs, so widespread that by the start of the seventh century, there were relics within or under all altars throughout the Western Church. The second Council of Nice was the first to demand this by law.

> We have decreed that all temples consecrated without the relics of martyrs must have sacred relics deposited therein, with the customary prayers. A bishop who hereafter consecrates a temple without relics is to be deposed, as being one who has transgressed ecclesiastical traditions.[5]

The strict features of this law of the East had little influence in the West, since it had been motivated by the Iconoclasts, who were a purely Eastern problem. General practices in the West were not so iron-clad that they could never suffer any exception. Thus it was that the second Council of Chelsea in England (in 816) looked upon the placing of relics as an important part of altar-consecration, but did not hesitate to say, nevertheless, that relics were not indispensable. If there were relics, they were to be interred; if there were none to be had, the Eucharist alone would suffice, "because it is the Body and Blood of Christ, our Lord."[6]

It was not until the year 1596, when Pope Clement VIII published the Roman Pontifical, that the general custom became a general law, and the placing of relics in every altar, fixed or portable, became an integral part of the consecration.[7] Even

---

[3] This law of the Council of Carthage was accepted by Gratian, and appears in his Decretum, c. 26, D. I, *de consecratione*. It has already been cited in this book on page 000. Cf. Braun, *Der Christliche Altar*, (2 vols., Munich, 1924), I, 540 for his evaluation of the decree.

[4] Bliley, *Altars*, p. 41.

[5] Can. 7—Mansi, XIII, 751.

[6] Hardouin, *Acta Conciliorum*, IV, 1220.

[7] Pontificale Romanum, titles: *De ecclesiae dedicatione seu consecratione; De altaris consecratione quae fit sine ecclesiae dedicatione; De altaris portatilis consecratione.*

after the Pontifical was printed and promulgated, theologians still disputed whether relics were essential for validity, or merely integral parts without which altars would still be validly consecrated.[8]

The question is now beyond all controversy, however, since the Congregation of Rites has stated in several decrees of comparatively recent date that altars without relics are not validly consecrated.[9] The Code of Canon Law has the same invalidating prescript for altars without relics, since Canon 1198 §4 says:

> Both in immovable altars and in sacred altar-stones, let there be, according to the norms of the liturgical laws, a sepulchre containing relics of the Saints, closed with a stone.

Consequently all contrary opinions which were probable before the Code have lost their value, and may not be followed in practice.[10]

The priest at Mass prays: *"Oramus te, Domine, per merita Sanctorum tuorum, quorum reliquiae hic sunt. . . ."* Consequently, the relics of the Blessed will not suffice for valid consecration, since the prayer refers explicitly to the relics of Saints. The relics of at least two Saints are to be placed in the altar or the altar-stone, but it is not necessary that both be martyrs, although the common and general practice is to have only martyrs' relics for the altars.[11] In a particular response to the bishop of Vilna, however, the Congregation of Rites stated that it was not necessary to have the relics of several martyrs for a valid consecration, since the relics of a martyr *and* a confessor or virgin sufficed, as did also the relics of one martyr alone.[12]

---

[8] De Lugo, *De Sacramento Eucharistiae*, disp. XX, sect. 3, n. 75, was the most important author holding that relics were required only for liceity. Cf. also Ferraris, v. *Altare*, art. I, n. 214; St. Alphonsus, *Theol. Mor.*, VI, 369 for discussion of the probability of the opposed opinions.

[9] S. R. C., *Rhedonen.*, Oct. 6 ,1837—*Decr. Auth.*, n. 2777; *Vivarien.*, Dec. 7, 1844—*Decr. Auth.*, n. 2876; *Sancti Flori*, May 23, 1846—*Decr. Auth.*, n. 2911; *Limburgen.*, Feb. 27, 1847—*Decr. Auth.*, n. 2941.

[10] Gasparri, *De Sanctissima Eucharistia*, (2 vols., Paris, 1897), I, n. 324; Augustine, *A Commentary*, VI, 90; Coronata, *De Locis et Temporibus Sacris*, p. 105.

[11] S. R. C., *Rhedonen.*, Oct. 6, 1837—*Decr. Auth.*, n. 2777.

[12] S. R. C., *Vilnen.*, Feb. 16, 1906—*Decr. Auth.*, n. 4180.

The Congregation has never stated whether a consecration of an altar with relics of confessors or virgins alone would be valid. Gasparri doubts the validity of such a consecration,[13] and Bliley says that the Holy See would have to be petitioned for a solution if such a case should happen.[14]

The relics which are placed in altars should be first-class, i.e., actual parts of the bodies of Saints.[15] Some authors deny this, asserting that second-class relics (i.e., parts of the garments or of the clothes of saints) suffice, because of the fact that the Congregation of Rites never stipulated any particular kind of relics, and because of the additional fact that in the early days of the Church such relics were placed within altars.[16] There is little doubt, however, that the ordinary practice at present demands first-class relics for all altars, and also that the law taken by Gratian into his *Decretum* no longer can be used to justify the placing of secondary relics in these days.[17]

When relics are placed in the cavity of a consecrated altar, the bishop puts them into a closed and sealed casket, together with a written certificate of the consecration, signed and dated:

> Ego N. Episcopus N. consecravi altare hoc, in honorem Sancti N., et reliquias sanctorum Martyrum N. et N. in eo inclusi. . . .[18]

In the consecration of a portable altar, the Pontifical does not require that this document be inserted, probably because of the smallness of the cavity.[19]

Relics placed in altars must be certainly authentic, never

---

13 *De. Ss. Eucharistia,* I, n. 327.

14 *Altars,* p. 84, note. 57.

15 Van der Stappen, *Sacra Liturgia,* III, 29; De Herdt, *Sacrae Liturgiae Praxis,* I, n. 178.

16 Many, *Praelectiones de Locis Sacris,* p. 208; Coronata, *De Locis et Temporibus Sacris,* p. 106; Augustine, *A Commentary,* VI, 91.

17 Bliley, *Altars,* p. 84, note 59: "This opinion [favoring secondary relics] seems to be supported by c. 26, D. I, *de consecr.*" It must be noted, however, that Gratian's decree is based on a fourth-century law which had been necessitated by excessive abuses in the erection of altars. Present conditions are not the same as in those times.

18 *Pontificale Romanum,* tit. *De Consecratione altaris quae fit sine ecclesiae dedicatione.*

19 *Pontificale Romanum,* tit. *De Altaris Portatilis consecratione.*

doubtful. They must be placed in the relic cavity of the altar, and covered with a small stone which is cemented to the altar-table.[20] Cement should not be used in place of a stone, else the altar is invalidly consecrated. If there is any such altar, the cement must be dug out, a stone then inserted in its place, and the altar re-consecrated.[21]

The altar does not lose its consecration if the seal (sigillum) around the relics is broken, unless the *sepulchrum* or relic-cavity is broken or altered.[22] Altars that had been opened by pastors in order to see whether there really were relics within must be considered as violated, and in need of a new consecration, even though the cavity had been immediately re-sealed.[23]

ART. II. PRIVILEGES OF A CHURCH WITH A NOTABLE RELIC

The following are notable relics: all relics of the True Cross or of the Passion; the whole body of a Saint, or the head, the arm, the forearm, the heart, head, hand, tongue, leg, or that part of the body in which the Saint suffered martyrdom—provided that it be entire and not small or minute.[24]

If a church possesses any such relic of a Saint whose name is in the Roman martyrology, all the priests attached to that church may say the proper Mass and Office of that Saint on his feast-day. The Credo is said at the Mass, either on the day of the Saint's martyrdom or of death.[25] Only the proper church receives the privilege; a cathedral church does not communicate it to others, nor do religious communicate it to others.[26] This feast is distinct and separate from the annual feast of the Commemoration of Holy Relics. Notable relics of the Beatified do

[20] S. R. C., *Scardonen.*, Sept. 7, 1630—*Decr. Auth.*, n. 542; *Bituricens.*, Dec. 8, 1851—*Decr. Auth.*, n. 2991.

[21] S. R. C., *Arichaten.*, July 28, 1883—*Decr. Auth.*, n. 3585.

[22] S. R. C., *Bituricensis*, Dec. 5, 1851—*Decr. Auth.*, n. 2991 ad 2.

[23] S. R. C., *Hippolyti*, Aug. 31, 1867—*Decr. Auth.*, n. 3162 ad V.

[24] Canon 1281, §2. Cf. also page 120 for discussion of notable relics.

[25] S. R. C., decretum generale, Jan. 10, 1693—*Decr. Auth.*, n. 1890. Cf. Herdt, *Sacrae Liturgiae Praxis*, II, n. 198.

[26] S. R. C., *Mexicana*, Nov. 20, 1677—*Decr. Auth.*, n. 1603 ad 1; *Urbis*, April 8, 1628—*Decr. Auth.*, n. 460 ad 2; *Galliarum*, Jan. 10, 1693—*Decr. Auth.*, n. 1890 ad 5.

not bring this privilege; nor do similar relics of Saints not named in the Roman Martyrology; nor do relics whose identity is unknown, or to whom has been assigned a conventional name by the act of "christening."[27] Unless the relic is notable, the special Mass and Office are not allowed—even though the relic be a *first-class* one.[28]

Clerics not bound to choir but who are attached to the church possessing the notable relic may participate in the privileges.[29] If the Saint whose notable relic is possessed has a feast-day jointly with another Saint who was not a blood-relation to him, his Office and Mass are separated from that of the companion Saint. In such cases the Mass and Office are from the Common.[30]

There is no obligation to use these privileges, however, and if it is so desired, they may be omitted.[31]

ART. III. MANNER OF PRESERVING RELICS

Relics should be kept in special cabinets or closets, under lock and key. They should not be left in the church habitually, even though they are hidden by veils or coverings.[32] They should be always kept sealed and enclosed in their reliquaries, which are blessed by the bishop according to the form in the Roman Ritual.[33] Pastors and custodians of churches should see to it that there is no irreverence done to the relics.[34] If there is no

---

[27] S. R. C., decr., Dec. 19, 1643—*Decr. Auth.*, n. 853; *Dubium*, June 3, 1662—*Decr. Auth.*, n. 1234 ad 1; *Ferrarien.*, June 7, 1681—*Decr. Auth.*, n. 1670; *Toletana*, Nov. 20, 1683—*Decr. Auth.*, n. 1722; *Caesenaten*, July 30, 1689—*Decr. Auth.*, n. 1811 ad 3; decr. gener., Jan. 10, 1693—*Decr. Auth.*, n. 1890; *Bituntina*, October 1, 1707—*Decr. Auth.*, n. 2180.

[28] S. R. C., *Ruben.*, Dec. 3, 1672—*Decr. Auth.*, n. 1460; *Barcinon*, April 11, 1840—*Decr. Auth.*, n. 2802 ad 1; *Patavina*, Dec. 7, 1844—*Decr. Auth.*, n. 2883 ad 1; *Cadurcen.*, March 11, 1871—*Decr. Auth.*, n. 3238.

[29] S. R. C., *Mexicana*, Nov. 20, 1677—*Decr. Auth.*, n. 1603 ad 2.

[30] S. R. C., *Resolutio Dubiorum*, June 20, 1899—*Decr. Auth.*, n. 4037.

[31] Herdt, *Praxis Sacrae Liturgiae*, II, q. 198.

[32] Mothon, *Institutiones Canoniques*, II, n. 2499; Haegy, *Manuel de Liturgie*, I, 690.

[33] *Rituale Romanum*, Appendix III, *Benedicenda ab Episcopo*. This blessing of reliquaries is reserved to the bishop, but he may delegate it to another cleric.

[34] Canon 1289, §2, as on page 111.

proper and distinctive place for them in the sacristy, such as a special closet or niche, the tabernacle of a side altar where the Blessed Sacrament is never reserved seems to be a fit place. They must never be placed in the main Tabernacle of the church, of course. It is not wrong to keep relics of the True Cross together with relics of the Saints. This is forbidden in public exposition, but not in private custody or retention.[35]

The relics should not be removed from their capse even for the sake of cleaning the reliquary, unless the Ordinary grant permission and also re-seal them in their container with his own stamp, impressed in wax. If the red-silk cords fastening the relics within the capse are broken, or if the glass cover be destroyed, the damage ought to be repaired at once. If the injury be such that the seal or the relics themselves must be tampered with in order to repair the injury, the local Ordinary must be petitioned for a new approval of the relics.[36] In this case, the Ordinary should affix his seal to the newly repaired reliquary, and at the same time fasten within the capse the other seal of the former authenticating Ordinary.[37] The documents for the authenticity of a relic should be carefully guarded. If they are lost or destroyed, petition should be sent to the authority who issued them so that a new document may be drawn up. If these documents are not had, the relic must not be placed in public exposition; even if the documents are had, the relic and the documents must be presented to the local Ordinary for an examination and approval before they are exhibited in public cult. As soon as the documents are lost, the relics must be taken from public veneration, and they may not be exposed again until new documents for their authenticity have been obtained. The local Ordinary, if he so desires, may issue a decree of temporary approval for them, provided there is certainty that the relics are genuine.

---

[35] *Acta Sanctae Sedis,* II (1866), 577; Van der Stappen, *Sacra Liturgia,* IV, q. 365; Mothon, *Inst. Canon.,* II, n. 2505.

[36] Morrisroe, "Custody and Veneration of Relics," *Irish Ecclesiastical Record,* XXII (1907), 537.

[37] Haegy, *Manuel de Liturgie,* I, 690; Mothon. *Inst. Canoniq.,* II, n. 2497.

ART. IV. EXPOSITION OF RELICS

A. *Place of Exposition.* Relics of the Saints may be placed on the altar, at each side of the central Crucifix. If there are many relics, they may be placed between the candelabra, on each side of the altar.[38] Relics of the True Cross or of the Passion should be given a more worthy place, i.e., in the middle of the altar. It is never allowed, however, to place any relics, even of the True Cross, on top of the Tabernacle or in front of the door of the Tabernacle. Neither is it allowed to expose relics on an altar where the Blessed Sacrament is exposed. In this latter case, relics may be exposed on a side altar of the same church, but they must not be offered to the veneration of the faithful as long as the Blessed Sacrament is exposed.[39] The reliquaries should not resemble too closely the monstrance in which the Blessed Sacrament is exposed; neither should reliquaries be placed on a throne in such a way that the ordinary faithful would think that the Blessed Sacrament was exposed.[40] There should not be a pall spread beneath exposed relics,[41] but there must always be at least two candles lighted.[42] The priest who offers or exposes the relics for veneration wears a surplice and stole, and is preceded by two clerics with lighted candles. A white stole is worn if the relics are of a Saint not a martyr; a red stole, if the relics are of a martyr or if many relics of Saints and martyrs are exposed simultaneously. For exposition of a relic of the True Cross, a red stole is worn.

B. *The Veneration of Relics, and formulae.* Only a priest may present relics of the Saints for the faithful to kiss.[43] The relics should be enclosed and covered inside a case, either with

---

[38] *Ceremoniale Episcoporum,* lib. I, cap. 12, n. 12; Van der Stappen, *Sacra Liturgia,* IV, q. 365.

[39] S. R. C., *Lauden.,* June 17, 1900—*Decr. Auth.,* n. 4059 ad 2; *Tridentina,* March 12, 1836—*Decr. Auth.,* n. 2740 ad 1; *Aquen.,* Sept. 2, 1741—*Decr. Auth.,* n. 2365 ad 1; *Ordinis Minorum,* Sept. 17, 1897—*Decr. Auth.,* n. 3966 ad 1.

[40] Van der Stappen, *Sacra Liturgia,* IV, q. 365.

[41] S. R. C., decr. April 7, 1832—*Decr. Auth.,* n. 2689 ad 3.

[42] S. R. C., *Congregationis Montis Coronae,* Jan. 22, 1701—*Decr. Auth.,* n. 2967 ad 9; *Briocen.,* Aug. 12, 1854—*Decr. Auth.,* n. 3029 ad 13; *Sancti Miniati,* March 20, 1869—*Decr. Auth.,* n. 3204.

[43] Van der Stappen, *Sacra Liturgia,* IV, q. 365.

a facing of glass or with the relics imbedded and hidden. The priest wears a surplice and stole as for the exposition of relics.

The priest holds the relic in his right hand, and in his left a small towel or cloth with which he cleanses the face of the reliquary after each individual has kissed it. In the act of kissing a relic, the faithful should be *standing*, not kneeling. If it is a relic of the True Cross, the kiss should be preceded by a genuflection.[44]

No formula of words is prescribed; by custom the following have been introduced in some places:

> *"Per merita et intercessionem Sancti . . . concedat tibi* (or *vobis*) *Dominus salutem et pacem."*

If the relic is of the True Cross, the formula is this:

> *"Per Crucem et Passionem suam concedat tibi* (or *vobis*) *salutem et pacem."*[45]

or—

> *"Per signum Crucis de inimicis nostris libera nos, Deus noster."*

It would be better to touch the reliquary to the cheek instead of to the lips in some cases, ". . . ne nauseam faciat."

C. *Incensing Relics.* Relics of the True Cross are incensed by three double swings of the censer, and other relics of the Saints are incensed with two swings. In both cases the celebrant blesses the incense.[46] The relic of the True Cross, if placed in the middle of the altar, is incensed at the same time as the main Crucifix on the altar.[47]

Before incensing relics of the Saints, only an inclination of the head is made; before incensing relics of the True Cross or of the Passion, a genuflection is made, as a mark of imperfect or relative *latria.*[48] If relics are exposed at Mass or Vespers, the cele-

---

[44] Van der Stappen, *loc. cit.*

[45] Haegy, *Manuel de Liturgie,* I, 690.

[46] Haegy, *Manuel de Liturgie,* I, p. 706, n. 380. S. R. C., *Montis Regalis,* March 20, 1869—*Decr. Auth.,* n. 3201 ad VII.

[47] S. R. C., *Mutinen.,* Sept. 23, 1837—*Decr. Auth.,* n. 2769 ad X; *Brixien.,* Sept. 15, 1736—*Decr. Auth.,* n. 2324; *Urbis,* June 9, 1899—*Decr. Auth.,* n. 4026 ad 1.

[48] S. R. C., *Lucionen.,* May 23, 1835—*Decr. Auth.,* n. 2722.

brant incenses them; but if they are on a side altar, they may be incensed only at Vespers, provided that there are candles burning before them.[49] The celebrant always stands when incensing relics.

D. *Benediction given with Relics.* After exposition or procession with a relic of the Cross or of the Saints, benediction with the relic is given. If it is a relic of the Cross or of the Passion, the benediction is prescribed; if it is a relic of the Saints, benediction is optional on the part of the priest. The different ceremonies are outlined here in brief.

1. *Benediction with Relics of the True Cross or of the Passion.* The officiating minister wearing a red stole with a surplice (and also a red cope if he so desire), genuflects before the relic. Rising, he puts incense into the thurible and incenses the relic with three double swings, after which he again genuflects and disposes of the thurible. Taking the red humeral veil about his shoulders, he genuflects, and takes hold of the reliquary in the same manner as the monstrance. In silence he makes the sign of the Cross over the faithful. No chant or prayer of any kind is said, nor is any bell rung, nor is the relic incensed. Replacing the relic, he puts off the veil.

On Good Friday the stole and cope must be black, but the veil should be purple. If the Bishop give benediction with a relic of the Cross, he removes both mitre and skull-cap.[50]

2. *Benediction with Relics of the Saints.* Practically the same rites are followed as in the former ceremony, with a few exceptions. The celebrant wears a red or white stole according to the quality of the Saint. In place of a genuflection, only an inclination of the head is made. If incense is used, the celebrant blesses it. The humeral veil is not worn at the actual blessing of the faithful.

---

[49] S. R. C., *Treviren.*, July 31, 1665—*Decr. Auth.*, n. 1322 ad 2.

[50] Van der Stappen, *Sacra Liturgia*, IV, q. 365, n. IV; Haegy, *Manuel*, I, 687. These ceremonies are founded upon decrees of the Congregation of Rites—*Brixien.*, Sept. 15, 1736—*Decr. Auth.*, n. 2324; *Lucionen.*, May 23, 1835—*Decr. Auth.*, n. 2722 ad 3; *Cenomanen.*, Feb. 18, 1843—*Decr. Auth.*, n. 2854. This last decree is the main source of all the laws on ceremonies with relics of the Cross. S. C. R., *Mutinen.*, Sept. 23, 1837—*Decr. Auth.*, n. 2769 ad X, allowed the cope to be worn wherever there was a custom.

In all ceremonies with relics of the Saints or of the Blessed Virgin, the use of incense is not prescribed. Local customs may be followed in this regard.[51]

E. *Processions with Relics.* To carry the relics of a Beatified person in procession a special indult of the Holy See is required, and it must be distinct from that allowing a special Mass and Office.[52] In processions with the relics of the Saints, the cleric highest in rank has the right to carry the reliquary. All who carry relics must have their heads uncovered, except the Bishop. He may retain his mitre until benediction with the relic is given.[53] When the relic is of the True Cross, all in procession must have heads uncovered.[54]

The relics of the Saints may not be carried in procession under a baldachino, but that honor is allowed to relics of the Cross.[55] At least four torches[56] are carried in these processions, unless all the clerics are carrying lighted candles. The relics are incensed before and after the procession. At the end of a procession with relics of the Saints, benediction with the relic may be given, but there is no obligation; if the relics are of the True Cross or of the Passion, benediction must be given.

In processions for the solemn translation of notable relics, the ecclesiastics who carry the relics must be vested in chasubles or dolmatics (white or red, according to the quality of the Saint).[57]

Whenever the Blessed Sacrament is carried in procession,

---

[51] Wuest, *Matters Liturgical,* n. 813; Van der Stappen, *op. cit.*, n. 365.

[52] Van der Stappen, *Sacra Liturgia,* IV, 358; Vermeersch-Creusen, *Epitome,* II, n. 614. These rules are based on decrees of the Roman Congregations. Cf. S. R. C., decretum, Sept. 27, 1659—*Decr. Auth.*, n. 1130 ad 11. This last was a decree issued by the Congregation with the approval of Pope Alexander VII, on the cult to be shown to those who are Beatified but not yet canonized.

[53] S. R. C., *Angren.*, Aug. 18, 1877—*Decr. Auth.*, n. 3434 ad 4; *Mutinen.*, Sept. 23, 1837—*Decr. Auth.*, n. 2769 ad IV.

[54] S. R. C., *Nucerina,* Jan. 23, 1649—*Decr. Auth.*, n. 918 ad 1; *Novae Firmanae,* Dec. 1, 1657—*Decr. Auth.*, n. 1043; *Caietana,* Sept. 25, 1688—*Decr. Auth.*, n. 1800; *Caietana,* Sept. 2, 1690—*Decr. Auth.*, n. 1841.

[55] S. R. C., *Ripana,* Aug. 22, 1744—*Decr. Auth.*, n. 2379 ad 2; *Decretum Generale,* May 27, 1826—*Decr. Auth.*, n. 2647. This latter decree is the main source of all liturgy on the cult of the True Cross.

[56] Van Der Stappen, *Sacra Liturgia,* IV, q. 359.

[57] *Rituale Romanum,* tit. IX, cap. 14.

relics of the Saints should not be carried.[58] Exceptions have been allowed, however, provided that there be a great distance between the relics and the Blessed Sacrament.[59]

---

[58] S. R. C., *Caesaraugustana,* March 23, 1593—*Decr. Auth.,* n. 28; *Veneta,* June 17, 1684—*Decr. Auth.,* n. 1731.

[59] Herdt, *Praxis Sacrae Liturgiae,* II, n. 195.

BIBLIOGRAPHY

1. SOURCES

Acta Apostolicae Sedis, Romae, 1909-.

Acta et Decreta Conciliorum Recentiorum (*Collectio Lacensis*), 7 vols., Friburgiae Brisgoviae, 1897.

Acta Sanctae Sedis, 41 vols., Romae, 1865-1908.

Bullarium Benedicti Papae XIV, 13 vols., Mechliniae, 1827.

Bullarium Romanum, 24 vols., Augustae Taurinorum, 1857-1872.

Bullarii Romani Continuatio, 14 vols., Prati, 1845-1854.

Codex Iuris Canonici, Romae, 1917.

Collectanea S. Congregationis de Propaganda Fide, 2 vols., Romae, 1907.

Corpus Iuris Canonici, 2 vols., Lipsiae, 1922.

Corpus Iuris Civilis, 3 vols., Berolini, 1928-1929.

Decreta Authentica Congregationis Sacrorum Rituum, 7 vols., Romae, 1912.

Decreta Authentica Sacrae Congregationis Indulgentiis Sacrisque Reliquiis Praepositae, ab anno 1668 ad annum 1882, edita iussu et auctoritate Ss. D. N. Leonis, Papae XIII, Ratisbonae, 1883.

Denziger, *Enchiridion Symbolorum et Definitionum,* Wiceburgi, 1865.

Mansi, J. D., *Sacrorum Conciliorum Nova et Amplissima Collectio,* 53 vols., Parisiis, 1901-1927.

Missale Romanum, ed. typ. Vaticana III, Ratisbonae, 1925.

Pontificale Romanum Summorum Pontificum, 3 vols., Mechliniae, 1895.

Rescripta Authentica Sacrae Congregationis Indulgentiis Sacrisque Reliquiis Praepositae, Ratisbonae, 1885.

Rituale Romanum, ed. typ., Romae, 1925.

Regesta Romanorum Pontificum, 12 vols., Berolini, 1908-1925.

2. WORKS OF REFERENCE

Acta Sanctorum, 54 vols., Antverpiae, 1643-1853.

Agricola, Franciscus, *Tractatus Orthodoxus de Sanctorum Ss. Reliquiis,* Coloniae, 1580.

Analecta Bollandiana, Brussels, 1882-.

Andreucci, *Hierarchia Ecclesiae in varias suas partes distributa et canonice-theologice exposita,* 3 vols., Romae, 1766.

Assemani, Joseph, *Bibliotheca Juris Orientalis Canonici et Civilis,* 3 vols., Romae, 1725-1728.

Avanzini, *De Constitutione "Apostolicae Sedis,"* Romae, 1872.

(Bachofen) Charles Augustine, O. S. B., *A Commentary on the New Code of Canon Law,* 2 ed., 8 vols., St. Louis, 1924.

Ballerini-Palmieri, *Opus Theologicum Morale,* 2 ed., 7 vols., Prati, 1894.
Barbier de Montault, *Oeuvres Complétes,* 8 vols., Paris, 1893.
Battifol, "La Science des Reliques et l'Archéologie Biblique," *Revue Biblique,* I (1892), 186-198.
Baudin, *Fetishism and Fetish Worshippers,* New York, 1885.
Beissel, *Die Verehrung der Heiligen und ihrer Reliquien in Deutschland bis zum beginne des 13 Jahrunderts,* 2 vols., Freiburg, 1890-1892.
Bellarmine, Robert, S. J., *Opera Omnia,* 4 vols., Mediolani, 1858.
Benedict XIV (Prosper Lambertini), *De Servorum Dei Beatificatione et Beatorum Canonizatione,* Prati, 1843.
Bergier, *Dictionnaire de Théologie,* 7 vols., Besançon, 1827.
Blat, *Commentarium Textus Codicis Juris Canonici,* 6 vols., Romae, 1921-1927.
Bliley, *Altars according to the Code of Canon Law,* Washington, 1927.
Boldetti, *Osservazioni sopra i cimiteri de' santi Martiri et antichi Cristiani di Roma,* Roma, 1720.
Bouvier, *Institutiones Theologicae,* 6 ed., 4 vols., Parisiis, 1850.
Bridgett, T. E., C. Ss. R., *History of the Holy Eucharist in Great Britain,* London, 1908.
Bucceroni, J., S. J., *Institutiones Theologiae Moralis,* 5 ed., 2 vols., Romae, 1908.
Cabrol-Leclercq, *Dictionnaire d'Archéologie Chrétienne et de Liturgie,* 9 vols., Paris, 1924-1930.
Capello, F., S. J., *De Curia Romana iuxta Reformationem a Pio X sapientissime inductam,* Romae, 1911.
Catholic Encyclopedia, New York, 1907-1914.
Cavalieri, *Opera Omnia Liturgica,* 5 vols., Venetiis, 1758.
Chevalier, Ulysses, *Étude Critique sur l'origine du Saint Suaire de Lirey-Chambéry-Turin,* Paris, 1900.
Cocchi, *Commentarium in Universum Codicem Iuris Canonici,* 7 vols., Taurinorum Augustae, 1925-1928.
Collin de Plancy, *Dictionnaire Critique des Reliques et des Images Miraculeuses,* 3 vols., Paris, 1821-1822.
Coronata, M. a, *De Locis et Temporibus Sacris,* Augustae Taurinorum, 1922.
Craisson, D., *Manuale Totius Iuris Canonici,* 4 ed., 4 vols., Pictavii, 1875.
D'Alès, *Dictionnaire Apologétique de la Foi Catholique,* 4 vols., Paris, 1925.
Damascene, St. John, *Treatise on the Holy Images,* translated by M. H. Allies, Philadelphia, 1898.
D'Annibale, *Summula Theologiae Moralis,* 5 ed., 3 vols., Romae, 1908.
De Buck, *De Phialis Rubricatis quibus Martyrum Romanorum sepulchra dignosci dicuntur Observationes,* Bruxellis, 1855.
De Combes, *The Finding of the Cross,* translated by L. Cappadelta, New York, 1907.
De Fleury, Rohault, *Mémoire sur les Instruments de la Passion,* Paris, 1870.

De Herdt, *Sacrae Liturgiae Praxis*, 7 ed., 3 vols., Lovanii, 1883.

Delehaye, S. J., *Legends of the Saints*, translated by V. M. Crawford, London, 1907.

Delehaye, S. J., *Les Origines du Culte des Martyres*, Bruxelles, 1917.

De Lugo, *Disputationes Scholasticae et Morales*, 2 ed., 8 vols., Parisiis, 1869.

De Rossi, *La Roma Sotterranea Cristiana*, 3 vols., Roma, 1864.

Devoti, *Institutiones Canonicae*, Romae, 1830.

Dictionnaire Pratique des Connaissances Religieuses, 5 ed., 4 vols., Paris, 1925-1927.

Duchesne, *Liber Pontificalis*, 2 vols., Paris, 1892.

Effer, U., "Reliquien," *Kirchenlexikon*, X, 1030-1040.

Encyclopedia Britannica, 11 ed., New York, 1910.

Encyclopedia of Religion and Ethics, 12 vols., New York, 1918-1922.

Fabretti, R., *Inscriptionum Antiquarum quae in Aedibus Paternis asservantur Explicatio et Additamentum*, Romae, 1699.

Ferraris, *Prompta Bibliotheca Canonica, Juridica, Moralis, Theologica, necnon Ascetica, Polemica, Rubricistica, Historica*, 9 vols., Romae, 1885-1899.

Ferreres, J., *Compendium Theologiae Moralis*, 13 ed., 2 vols., Barcinone. 1925.

Ferreres, J., *Institutiones Canonicae*, 2 ed., 2 vols., Barcinone, 1920.

Fulda, *Das Kreuz und die Kreuzigung*, Breslau, 1878.

Garetius, Joannes, *De Sanctorum Invocatione Liber*, Gandavi, 1570.

Gasparri, *Tractatus Canonicus de Sanctissima Eucharistia*, 2 vols., Paris, 1897.

Genicot-Salsmans, *Institutiones Theologiae Moralis*, 10 ed., 2 vols., Bruxellis, 1022.

Gihr, N., *The Holy Sacrifice of the Mass*, St. Louis, 1902.

Goschler, *Dictionnaire Encyclopédique de la Théologie Catholique*, 3 ed., 26 vols., Paris, 1870.

Grandclaude, E., *Jus Canonicum*, 3 vols., Parisiis, 1882.

Guibert de Nogent, *De Sanctis et Eorum Pignoribus*, Migne *Patrologia Latina*, CLVI, 611-680.

Guiraud, "Commerce des Reliques," *Mélanges de Rossi*, Rome, 1892.

Guiraud, *Questions d'Histoire et d'Archéologie Chrétienne*, Paris, 1906.

Haddan, A. W., and W. Stubbs, *Councils and Ecclesiastical Documents Relating to Great Britain and Ireland*, 3 vols., London, 1871.

Halusa, Tezelin, "Kreuzreliquien," *Theologisch-praktische Quartalschrift* (Linz, 1832-), LXXIV (1921), 52-59.

Harduin, Jean S. J., *Acta Conciliorum et Epistulae, Decretales ac Constitutiones Summorum Pontificum*, 12 vols., Parisiis, 1725.

Harnack. *History of Dogma*, translated by N. Buchanan, 7 vols., Boston, 1897.

Hefele, J. C., *Histoire des Conciles d'apres les Documents Originaux*, 16 vols., Paris, 1907-1921.

Honoratus a Sancta Maria, *Animadversiones in Regulas et Usum Critices*, 3 vols., Venetiis, 1840.

Lacroix, Claudius, S. J., *Theologia Moralis*, 2 ed., 4 vols., Parisiis, 1867.

Laurentius, Joseph, *Institutiones Iuris Ecclesiastici*, Friburgi Brisgoviae, 1914.

Leclercq, "La Sainte Larme," *Dictionnaire d'Archéologie Chrétienne et de Liturgie*, VIII, cols. 1382-1393.

Leech, *A Comparative Study of the Constitution "Apostolicae Sedis" and the Codex Iuris Canonici*, Washington, 1922.

Lefranc, Abel, "Le Traité des Reliques de Guibert de Nogent," *Études d'Histoire du Moyen Âge*, Paris, 1896.

Lehmkuhl, S. J., *Theologia Moralis*, 12 ed., 2 vols., Friburgi Brisgoviae, 1914.

Leibnitz, G. W. von, *System of Theology*, translated by C. W. Russell, London, 1850.

Le Vavasseur-Haegy, *Manuel de Liturgie et Ceremonial selon le Rit Romain*, 10 ed., 2 vols., Paris, 1910.

Ligouri, St. Alphonsus, *Theologia Moralis*, 10 vols., Mechliniae, 1842-1845.

Lucius, *Les Origines du Culte des Saints dans l'Église Chrétienne*, Paris, 1908.

Mabillon, *Acta Ss. Ordinis S. Benedicti*, 6 vols., Venetiis, 1733.

Mabillon, *Eusebii Romani Epistola ad Theophilum Gallum, De Cultu Sanctorum Ignotorum*, Paris, 1698.

Mabillon, *Lettre d'un Bénédictin à M. l'Évêque de Blois, touchant le discernement des anciennes Reliques, au sujet d'une Dissertation de M. Thiers contre le sainte Larme de Vendôme*, Paris, 1700.

Marucchi, M. O., *Éléments d'Archéologie Chrétienne*, Paris, 1899.

Marucchi, M. O., *The Evidences of the Catacombs*, London, 1929.

Mioni, *Il Culto delle Relique*, Torino, 1908.

Migne, *Patrologiae Graecae Cursus Completus* (*MPG*), Parisiis, 1856-1864.

Migne, *Patrologia Latina* (*MPL*), Parisiis, 1847-1851.

Mocchegiani, Peter, O. F. M., *Jurisprudentia Ecclesiastica*, 3 vols., Friburgi Brisgoviae, 1905.

Mothon, Joseph, O. P., *Institutions Canoniques*, 2 vols., Paris, 1922.

Murray, Patrick, *Tractatus de Veneratione et Invocatione Sanctorum, et Veneratione Reliquiarum et Imaginum*, Dublin, 1881.

Noldin-Schönegger, *De Censuris*, Oenipotente, 1926.

Northcote, J. Spencer, *The Roman Catacombs*, Philadelphia, 1857.

Northcote-Brownlow, *Roma Sotterranea*, London, 1869.

Ojetti, B., S. J., *De Romana Curia*, Romae, 1910.

Ojetti, B., S. J., *Synopsis Rerum Moralium et Juris Pontificii*, 3 ed., 4 vols., Romae, 1912.

Perrone, Joannes, S. J., *Praelectiones Theologicae*, 3 vols., Parisiis, 1856.

Pfister, *Der Reliquienkult in Altertum*, Leipzig, 1909.

Prümmer, O. P., *Manuale Theologiae Moralis*, 3 vols., Friburgi, 1927.

Reiffenstuel, Anicletus, O. F. M., *Jus Canonicum Universum,* 7 vols., Parisiis, 1870.
Sole, *De Delictis et Poenis,* Romae, 1920.
Sporer-Bierbaum, *Theologia Moralis,* 2 ed., 3 vols., Paderbornae, 1901.
Suarez, *Opera Omnia,* 26 vols., Parisiis, 1861.
Thiers, *Dissertation sur le Sainte Larme de Vendôme, avec le Réponse à la lettre du Pere Mabillon touchant la pretendue Sainte Larme de Vendôme,* Amsterdam, 1751.
Thiers, *Traité des Superstitions qui regardent les Sacraments,* 4 ed., 4 vols., Paris, 1741.
Thomas, St., *Summa Theologica,* 10 vols., Romae, 1773.
Thurston, Herbert, S. J., "Relics," *Catholic Encyclopedia,* XII.
Thurston, Herbert, S. J., "Relics, Authentic and Spurious," *The Month,* May and June, 1930.
Vacant-Mangenot, *Dictionnaire de Théologie Catholique,* Paris, 1923-.
Vermeersch-Creusen, *Epitome Iuris Canonici,* 3 ed., 3 vols., Mechliniae, 1927.
Wernz, Franciscus, S. J., *Ius Decretalium,* 6 vols., Romae, 1906-1913.
Zallwein, G., *Principia Iuris Ecclesiastici,* 4 vols., Augustae Vind. et Oeniponti, 1763.

3. PERIODICALS

American Ecclesiastical Review, Philadelphia, 1889-.
Analecta Iuris Pontificii, Romae-Parisiis, 1855-1890.
Archiv für katholisches Kirchenrecht, Mainz, 1862-.
Il Monitore Ecclesiastico.
Irish Ecclesiastical Record, Dublin, 1864-.
Theologisch-praktische Quartalschrift, Linz, 1832-.

UNIVERSITAS CATHOLICA AMERICAE

WASHINGTONII, D. C.

FACULTAS IURIS CANONICI

No. 70

1931

DEUS LUX MEA

TITULI

QUOS

AD DOCTORATUS GRADUM

IN

IURE CANONICO

APUD UNIVERSITATEM CATHOLICAM AMERICAE

CONSEQUENDUM

PUBLICE PROPUGNABIT

EUGENIUS A. DOOLEY

SACERDOS E CONGREGATIONE

OBLATORUM MARIAE IMMACULATAE

IURIS CANONICI LICENTIATUS

HORA IX A. M. DIE XXVI MAII MCMXXXI

TITULI

IN IURE CANONICO

I.	De Dissertatione.	
II.	De Historia Iuris Canonici.	
III.	Canones 1-7	De Ambitu Codicis.
IV.	Canones 8-24	De Legibus Ecclesiasticis.
V.	Canones 25-30	De Consuetudine.
VI.	Canones 31-35	De Temporis Supputatione.
VII.	Canones 36-62	De Rescriptis.
VIII.	Canones 63-79	De Privilegiis.
IX.	Canones 80-86	De Dispensationibus.
X.	Canones 87-107	Generales Notiones de Personis.
XI.	Canones 111-117	De Clericorum Adscriptione Alicui Dioecesi.
XII.	Canones 118-123	De Iuribus et Privilegiis Clericorum.
XIII.	Canones 124-144	De Obligationibus Clericorum.
XIV.	Canones 145-195	De Officiis Ecclesiasticis.
XV.	Canones 196-210	De Potestate Ordinaria et Delegata.
XVI.	Canones 487-498	De Notione Religionis, et de Erectione et Suppressione Religionis, Provinciae, Domus.
XVII.	Canones 499-537	De Religionum Regimine.
XVIII.	Canones 538-586	De Admissione in Religionem.
XIX.	Canones 673-681	De Societatibus sive Virorum sive Mulierum in Communi Viventium sine Votis.
XX.	Canones 1012-1018	De Matrimonio in Genere.
XXI.	Canones 1019-1034	De Iis quae Matrimonii Celebrationi Praemitti debent.
XXII.	Canones 1035-1057	De Impedimentis in Genere.
XXIII.	Canones 1058-1066	De Impedimentis Impedientibus.
XXIV.	Canones 1067-1080	De Impedimentis Dirimentibus.
XXV.	Canones 1081-1093	De Consensu Matrimoniali.
XXVI.	Canones 1552-1568	De Notione Iudicii et de Foro Competenti.
XXVII.	Canones 1569-1607	De Variis Tribunalium Gradibus et Speciebus.
XXVIII.	Canones 1608-1645	De Disciplina in Tribunalibus Servanda.
XXIX.	Canones 1646-1666	De Partibus in Causa.
XXX.	Canones 1667-1705	De Actionibus et Exceptionibus.
XXXI.	Canones 1706-1725	De Causae Introductione.

XXXII.	Canones 1726-1746	De Litis Contestatione, de Litis Instantia, et de Interrogationibus Partibus in Iudicio Faciendis.
XXXIII.	Canones 1747-1836	De Probationibus.
XXXIV.	Canones 1837-1857	De Causis Incidentibus.
XXXV.	Canones 1858-1877	De Processus Publicatione, de Conclusione in Causa, de Causae Discussione, et de Sententia.
XXXVI.	Canones 1879-1891	De Appellatione.
XXXVII.	Canones 1902-1907	De Re Iudicata et de Restitutione in Integrum.
XXXVIII.	Canones 1960-1992	De Causis Matrimonialibus.
XXXIX.	Canones 2195-2198	De Natura Delicti eiusque Divisione.
XL.	Canones 2199-2211	De Imputabilitate Delicti, de Causis illam Aggravantibus vel Minuentibus, et de Iuridicis Delicti Effectibus.
XLI.	Canones 2212-2213	De Conatu Delicti.
XLII.	Canones 2214-2240	De Poenis in Genere.
XLIII.	Canones 2241-2285	De Poenis Medicinalibus seu de Censuris.
XLIV.	Canones 2286-2305	De Poenis Vindicativis.
XLV.	Canones 2306-2313	De Remediis Poenalibus et Poenitentiis.

IN IURE ROMANO

XLVI. The Periods of Roman Law.
XLVII. The Sources of Roman Law.
XLVIII. Personality.
XLIX. Slavery.
L. Citizenship.
LI. Patria Potestas.
LII. Personae in Manu.
LIII. Tutela et Cura.
LIV. Personae in Mancipio.
LV. Ownership.
LVI. De Obligationibus in Genere.
LVII. De Obligationibus Extra-Contractualibus.
LVIII. Furtum.
LIX. Damnum Injuria Datum.
LX. Injuria.

Vidit Facultas:

VALENTINUS T. SCHAAF, O.F.M., J.C.D., Vice-Decanus.
LUDOVICUS H. MOTRY, S.T.D., J.C.D., a Secretis.
FRANCISCUS J. LARDONE, S.T.D., J.U.D.

Vidit Rector Magnificus Universitatis:

JACOBUS HUGO RYAN, S.T.D., Ph.D., LL.D., Litt.D.

VITA

Eugene Aloysius Dooley was born in Lowell, Massachusetts, on September 7, 1901. He attended the Immaculate Conception parochial school, Lowell High School, and Canisius College, Buffalo, N. Y. In September, 1920, he entered the Novitiate of the Oblates of Mary Immaculate, at Tewksbury, Mass., and in the following September began philosophical and theological studies at the Oblate Scholasticate, Washington, D. C. On April 29, 1927, he was ordained to the priesthood, and served the following year as a parochial assistant in the Immaculate Conception Church, at Lowell, Mass. In the fall of 1928, he was transferred to the Oblate Scholasticate, Washington, D. C., and began graduate studies in the School of Canon Law at the Catholic University.

CATHOLIC UNIVERSITY OF AMERICA

CANON LAW STUDIES

1. Freriks, Rev. Celestine A., C.PP.S., J.C.D., Religious Congregations in Their External Relations, 121 pp., 1916.
2. Galliher, Rev. Daniel M., O.P., J.C.D., Canonical Elections, 117 pp., 1917.
3. Borkowski, Rev. Aurelius L., O.F.M., J.C.D., De Confraternitatibus Ecclesiasticis, 136 pp., 1918.
4. Castillo, Rev. Cayo, J.C.D., Disertacion Historico-canonica sobre la Potestad del Cabildo en Sede Vacante o Impedida del Vicario Capitular, 99 pp., 1919 (1918).
5. Kubelbeck, Rev. William J., S.T.B., J.C.D., The Sacred Penitentiaria and Its Relations to Faculties of Ordinaries and Priests, 129 pp., 1918.
6. Petrovits, Rev. Joseph J. C., S.T.D., J.C.D., The New Church Law on Matrimony, X-461 pp., 1919.
7. Hickey, Rev. John J., S.T.B., J.C.D., Irregularities and Simple Impediments in the New Code of Canon Law, 100 pp., 1920.
8. Klekotka, Rev. Peter J., S.T.B., J.C.D., Diocesan Consultors, 179 pp., 1920.
9. Wannenmacher, Rev. Francis, J.C.D., The Evidence in Ecclesiastical Procedure Affecting the Marriage Bond, 1920. (Not Printed.)
10. Golden, Rev. Henry Francis, J.C.D., Parochial Benefices in the New Code, IV-119 pp., 1921. (Printed 1925.)
11. Koudelka, Rev. Charles J., J.C.D., Pastors, Their Rights and Duties According to the New Code of Canon Law, 211 pp., 1921.
12. Melo, Rev. Antonius, O.F.M., J.C.D., De Exemptione Regularium, X-188 pp., 1921.
13. Schaaf, Rev. Valentine Theodore, O.F.M., S.T.B., J.C.D., The Cloister, X-180 pp., 1921.
14. Burke, Rev. Thomas Joseph, S.T.B., J.C.D., Competence in Ecclesiastical Tribunals, IV-117 pp., 1922.
15. Leech, Rev. George Leo, J.C.D., A Comparative Study of the Constitution "Apostolicae Sedis" and the "Codex Juris Canonici," 179 pp., 1922.
16. Motry, Rev. Hubert Louis, S.T.D., J.C.D., Diocesan Faculties according to the Code of Canon Law, II-167 pp., 1922.
17. Murphy, Rev. George Lawrence, J.C.D., Delinquencies and Penalties in the Administration and the Reception of the Sacraments, IV-121 pp., 1923.

18. O'Reilly, Rev. John Anthony, S.T.B., J.C.D., Ecclesiastical Sepulture in the New Code of Canon Law, II-129 pp., 1923.
19. Michalicka, Rev. Wenceslas Cyrill, O.S.B., J.C.D., Judicial Procedure in Dismissal of Clerical Exempt Religious, 107 pp., 1923.
20. Dargin, Rev. Edward Vincent, S.T.B., J.C.D., Reserved Cases According to the Code of Canon Law, IV-103 pp., 1924.
21. Godfrey, Rev. John A., S.T.B., J.C.D., The Right of Patronage According to the Code of Canon Law, 153 pp., 1924.
22. Hagedorn, Rev. Francis Edward, J.C.D., General Legislation on Indulgences, II-154 pp., 1924.
23. King, Rev. James Ignatius, J.C.D., The Administration of the Sacraments to Dying Non-Catholics, V-141 pp., 1924.
24. Winslow, Rev. Francis Joseph, A.F.M., J.C.D., Vicars and Prefects Apostolic, IV-149 pp., 1924.
25. Correa, Rev. Jose Servelion, S.T.L., J.C.D., La Potestad Legislativa de la Iglesia Catolica, IV-127 pp., 1925.
26. Dugan, Rev. Henry Francis, M.A., J.C.D., The Judiciary Department of the Diocesan Curia, 87 pp., 1925.
27. Keller, Rev. Charles Frederick, S.T.B., J.C.D., Mass Stipends, 167 pp., 1925.
28. Paschang, Rev. John Linus, J.C.D., The Sacramentals According to the Code of Canon Law, 129 pp., 1925.
29. Piontek, Rev. Cyrillus, O.F.M., S.T.B., J.C.D., De Indulto Exclaustrationis necnon Saecularizationis, XIII-289 pp., 1925.
30. Kearney, Rev. Richard Joseph, S.T.B., J.C.D., Sponsors at Baptism According to the Code of Canon Law, IV-127 pp., 1925.
31. Bartlett, Rev. Chester Joseph, A.M., LL.B., J.C.D., The Tenure of Parochial Property in the United States of America, V-108 pp., 1926.
32. Kilker, Rev. Adrian Jerome, J.C.D., Extreme Unction, V-425 pp., 1926.
33. McCormick, Rev. Robert Emmett, J.C.D., Confessors of Religious, VIII-266 pp., 1926.
34. Miller, Rev. Newton Thomas, J.C.D., Founded Masses According to the Code of Canon Law, VII-93 pp., 1926.
35. Roelker, Rev. Edward G., S.T.D., J.C.D., Principles of Privilege According to the Code of Canon Law, XI-166 pp., 1926.
36. Bakalarczyk, Rev. Richardus, M.I.C., J.U.D., De Novitiatu, VIII-208 pp., 1927.
37. Pizzuti, Rev. Lawrence, O.F.M., J.U.L., De Parochis Religiosis, 1927. (Not Printed.)
38. Bliley, Rev. Nicholas Martin, O.S.B., J.C.D., Altars According to the Code of Canon Law, XIX-132 pp., 1927.
39. Brown, Brendan Francis, A.B., LL.M., J.U.D., The Canonical Juristic Personality with Special Reference to its Status in the United States of America, V-212 pp., 1927.
40. Cavanaugh, Rev. William Thomas, C.P., J.U.D., The Reservation of the Blessed Sacrament, VIII-101 pp., 1927.

41. Doheny, Rev. William J., C.S.C., A.B., J.U.D., Church Property: Modes of Acquisition, X-118 pp., 1927.

42. Feldhaus, Rev. Aloysius H., C.PP.S., J.C.D., Oratories, IX-141 pp., 1927.

43. Kelly, Rev. James Patrick, A.B., J.C.D., The Jurisdiction of the Simple Confessor, X-208 pp., 1927.

44. Neuberger, Rev. Nicholas J., J.C.D., Canon 6 or the Relation of the Codex Juris Canonici to the Preceding Legislation, V-95 pp., 1927.

45. O'Keeffe, Rev. Gerald Michael, J.C.D., Matrimonial Dispensations, Powers of Bishops, Priests, and Confessors, VIII-232 pp., 1927.

46. Quigley, Rev. Joseph, A.M., A.B., J.C.D., Condemned Societies, 139 pp., 1927.

47. Zaplotnik, Rev. Ioannes Leo, J.C.D., De Vicariis Foraneis, X-142, 1927.

48. Duskie, Rev. John Aloysius, A.B., J.C.D., The Canonical Status of the Orientals in the United States, VIII-196 pp., 1928.

49. Hyland, Rev. Francis Edward, J.C.D., Excommunication, Its Nature, Historical Development and Effects, VIII-181 pp., 1928.

50. Reinmann, Rev. Gerald Joseph, O.M.C., J.C.D., The Third Order Secular of Saint Francis, 201 pp., 1928.

51. Schenk, Rev. Francis J., J.C.D., The Matrimonial Impediments of Mixed Religion and Disparity of Cult. XVI-318 pp., 1929.

52. Coady, Rev. John Joseph, S.T.D., J.U.D., A.M., The Appointment of Pastors, VIII-150 pp., 1929.

53. Kay, Rev. Thomas Henry, J.C.D., Competence in Matrimonial Procedure, VIII-164 pp., 1929.

54. Turner, Rev. Sidney Joseph, C.P., J.U.D., The Vow of Poverty. XLIX-217 pp., 1929.

55. Kearney, Rev. Raymond A., A.B., S.T.D., J.C.D., The Principles of Delegation, VII-149 pp., 1929.

56. Conran, Rev. Edward James, A.B., J.C.D., The Interdict, V-163 pp., 1930.

57. O'Neill, Rev. William H., J.C.D., Papal Rescripts of Favor, VII-219 pp., 1930.

58. Bastnagel, Rev. Clement Vincent, J.U.D., The Appointment of Parochial Adjutants and Assistants, XV-262 pp., 1930.

59. Ferry, Rev. William A., A.B., J.C.D., Stole Fees, X-108 pp., 1930.

60. Costello, Rev. John Michael, A.B., J.C.D., Domicile and Quasi-Domicile, VII-201 pp., 1930.

61. Kremer, Rev. Michael Nicholas, A.B., S.T.D., J.C.D., Church Support in the United States, VI-137 pp., 1930.

62. Angulo, Rev. Luis, C.M., J.C.L., Legislación de la Iglesia Católica sobre la intención en la aplicación de la Misa, 1931.

63. Frey, Rev. Wolfgang, O.S.B., A.B., J.C.L., The Act of Religious Profession, 1931.

64. ROBERTS, REV. JAMES BRENDAN, A.B., J.C.L., The Banns of Marriage, 1931.
65. RYDER, REV. RAYMOND ALOYSIUS, A.B., J.C.L., Simony, 1931.
66. CAMPAGNA, REV. MICHAEL ANGELO, Ph.B., J.U.L., Il Vicario Generale del Vescovo, 1931.
67. COX, REV. JOSEPH GODFREY, A.B., J.C.L., The Administration of Seminaries, 1931.
68. GREGORY, REV. DONALD JOSEPH, S.T.B., J.U.L., The Pauline Privilege, 1931.
69. DONOHUE, REV. JOHN FRANCIS, A.M., J.C.L., The Impediment of Crime, 1931.
70. DOOLEY, REV. EUGENE, O.M.I., J.C.L., Church Law on Sacred Relics, 1931.

CPSIA information can be obtained
at www.ICGtesting.com
Printed in the USA
LVHW110410100620
657013LV00002B/46